Apostle of the East

The Life and Journeys of Daniel Little

Russell M. Lawson

WIPF & STOCK · Eugene, Oregon

Wipf and Stock Publishers
199 W 8th Ave, Suite 3
Eugene, OR 97401

Apostle of the East
The Life and Journeys of Daniel Little
By Lawson, Russell M.
Copyright©2019 by Lawson, Russell M.
ISBN 13: 978-1-5326-9474-5
Publication date 6/20/2019
Previously published by St. Polycarp Publishing House, 2019

DEDICATION

For the men of the Brotherhood of St. Andrew
St. John's Episcopal Church
Tulsa, Oklahoma

Portrait of Daniel Little
Courtesy of the Unitarian Universalist Church, Kennebunk, Maine

CONTENTS

1	The Whistle	1
2	Pastor Little	8
3	Explorer on a Mission	24
4	The Pious Scientist	71
5	The Highest Peak	99
6	Missionary to the Penobscots	121
7	Apostle of the East	141
8	Final Journey	161
	Sources Consulted	186
	Maps	194
	Index	198
	About the Author	204

He was an earnest, vigilant, industrious and faithful watchman over the great interests of humanity; a true disciple of his Lord and Master.

- Bourne, History of Wells and Kennebunk

1 THE WHISTLE

Humans are subject to the tyranny of time. At a single moment, a person's life changes, takes a different direction than that heretofore. Humans try to track such instances, narrow them to a specific date, time of day, hour and minute, to attempt to exert some feeble control over what is uncontrollable. Other instances cannot be dated, are not subject to clocks and calendars. They just happen, vaguely but definitively.

At such a moment, Daniel Little was walking along the road returning home from the port, where he had journeyed earlier that day to inquire about a shipment of furniture he had been expecting. His business concluded, he departed for the two mile walk along the Port Road back to the parsonage, where he and his wife and children lived in a small village called Kennebunk. Little had lived in Kennebunk for half a dozen years, having accepted the call of the Second Parish in 1751 to minister to their needs. He had in 1752 built a snug two-story dwelling on the outskirts of the village on the road to the port. The Kennebunk River was just north of his home. He had a fine garden, a quiet life, a stable existence, and considered himself happy, blessed by God.

Little was a native of Newburyport, Massachusetts, and had grown up in nearby Haverhill. He had been well-educated by private tutors and had become a gifted Gospel minister. He arrived in Maine at a time between wars, when there appeared to be a modicum of peace, the previous conflict, King George's War, having been concluded a few years earlier. The inhabitants of Maine had, unlike some

British-American settlements in North America, generally been spared the worst of recent warfare. Rarely did Maine homesteaders fear for their lives from attacking French and, particularly, their Abenaki allies. Indeed the British had been on the offensive against Indian tribes and the French during King George's War, and the Indians had the worst of it. Likewise when war broke out again in 1755, Maine seacoast communities were largely spared the violence that others further west and south experienced. There was, then, during the French-Indian War, a slight sense of security in Maine seacoast communities that previous generations would have hardly felt.

Daniel Little was walking alone this day on the road from the port, approaching a bridge crossing a tidal inlet, feeling full and satisfied, his thoughts wandering about his favorite themes—the wonderful plenty of the land; the rich fodder, marsh hay, bending in the breeze; the cool, moist air promising much for the farm community; God's benevolence revealed in nature—when a sudden noise interrupted his solitude. A whistle. Not the whistle of a gull or hawk, or the whistle of the wind blowing through birches and pines. Rather an artificial whistle made by a contrived instrument. Little had heard the pewter and wood whistles used by militiamen on training days, but this one somehow sounded different, ominous. There was no militia training that day. All was quiet save the brief shrill of the whistle. Uncertain, afraid and cautious, Little slipped from the road and hid in the tall marsh grasses next to the bridge support. A whistle implied at least two separate warriors or warrior-bands. Had they seen him? Were they coming even now to capture him? He thought of his family, his widowed wife, his fatherless children. Even if the raiders had not seen him, they would use the road, cross the bridge, as he had. Little, knowing he must depart quickly, crawled on his hands and knees in the shallow, rank water of the marsh, provided by the grace of God to protect him; he moved slowly away from the bridge. He heard soft footsteps. He glimpsed a warrior. Stories from the past descended upon him.

A child in Haverhill, growing up during Dummer's War, when there was so much talk of militia hunting scalps, paid for by the Province of Massachusetts according to the age and gender of the deceased; listening to the bravado of the soldiers mixed with the fear in peoples' voices of the savagery of the enemy, of the barbarism, of how they treated defenseless children and women, though they learned their lesson when they captured the likes of Hannah Duston during King William's War, who paid them back fully, taking their scalps and bringing them to Haverhill. Indians and French attacked the town again in Queen Anne's War, just a dozen years before Little's birth. Other towns besides Haverhill—such as Deerfield, Dover, Oyster River, Salmon Falls, York—in Massachusetts, New Hampshire, and Maine experienced the silent incursions of the enemy, the killing of the innocent, the capture of women and children. The people of the time considered the Indians worse than dogs. Ministers in the pulpit condemned them as agents of the Enemy. They were a silent, nefarious force of evil, unexpected, merciless.

The warriors Little saw, if he got a good look, were scantily clad save for a breech-cloth and moccasins and leggings reaching to the upper thigh, but nothing about the stomach and chest. They were strong, tattooed, their head shaved except for a scalp-lock. They were armed with bow and arrow, or a musket, and a war ax with a stone or iron head. The minister crawled along the narrow tidal channels that marked the marshland, which allowed him to go undetected. He made his way in a westerly direction for a long time until he no longer heard the sounds of men, and feeling that he had escaped the immediate danger, quickly rushed back to the parsonage, paralleling the road, fearing the worst, praying for the best.

Little found that all was well. Indeed the raiders had come and gone without attacking anyone; all in the community were saved. But something had changed in the mind of the pastor. The peace that he had felt before the incident had vanished with the raiders. Little kept his possessions, family, friends, and life, but not his peace. There was now a blot on contentment. The presence of evil, Little knew from the Bible, is constant, ubiquitous—but hitherto he had rarely known it. Evil was theoretical, something to be talked about, a theological concept, like Adam and Eve's sin, a distant reality that never quite penetrated the body and mind. Evil, like God, transcends the moment, and though Little was aware of its existence, he had never felt it overwhelm the present. Until now. Evil is present, possible at any moment.

He could never rid himself of the sound of the whistle.

***

Daniel Little became, within twenty years, the Apostle of the East—so-called by his contemporaries and admirers for his many journeys along Maine's eastern frontier to minister to English settlers and the Indians particularly of the Penobscot valley. Little made repeated journeys before and after America's War for Independence. He was a restless adventurer, a messenger for Christ. So many of his ilk, the hundreds of Protestant clergymen of small New England towns, never ventured forth; they were content to stay put, to battle sin among their own neighbors, to shepherd the flock in the daily cares of life, to administer the sacraments of baptism and communion, to teach and preach, counsel and condole. Little did all of these as well during his long tenure as pastor of the Second Parish of Wells, Maine—what became the First Parish of Kennebunk. He served the people for over fifty years. But all of this activity as a pastor, the responsibilities of a large family, the intellectual demands on a Christian minister, were insufficient. Little felt compelled to do more.

Daniel Little became a member of the Society for Propagating the Gospel, founded by New England clergy in the late 1780s. Like many of the members of this missionary organization, Little tended toward a liberal Protestant theology in which he reached out to others through good works more than theological prescriptions. After the defeat of France in 1763, there was a religious and power vacuum in the Penobscot valley; the native Penobscot tribe, like many Maine Algonquians, had been converted by the French Catholics. Little, impatient with what he considered to be the flimsy theology of the *Papists*, wanted to bring to the Penobscots a love and devotion for the Gospel. At the same time, English settlers of the eastern frontier generally lacked contact with Gospel ministers, and were hungry for the rich milk of the Word. Both of these groups, Indians and frontier settlers, living in religious limbo, required not just the Gospel but the accoutrements of religious society as well. It was not sufficient, as the Catholics believed, to merely convert: the people must embrace the Christian lifestyle, that is, Christian civilization. Little, not a religious theoretician, rather a practical preacher, sought as a pastor and missionary to spread *social happiness*—a pastoral Christianity fit for an agrarian people.

Daniel Little like many of his contemporaries combined the roles of clergyman and scientist; his particular interests were in the physical and life sciences and metallurgy. Little was a student of *Elder Scripture*, of God's reason and benevolence written into nature. God, he believed, provided humans with *hints* by which they could use the wonderful plenty of nature to thrive. Little's simple piety in a God who blesses all of the Creation led him to move increasingly away from New England Calvinism to a more Universalist mindset. Feeling that anyone can be saved spurred Little on to bring the Good News to the ignorant, the wayward, the Catholic, the Indian.

Little's interest in natural history encouraged him to keep journals of his travels, in which he recorded his itinerary, those with whom he met, the landscape in which he traveled, and his observations of the remarkable of nature and humankind. He made six extensive journeys, of which he kept detailed diaries of five, which provides a window into a past time when the settlements of the eastern frontier and Penobscot valley were rustic and few and far between. Little braved mountains, rivers, foggy bays, isolated islands, barrenness and loneliness, and inhospitable conditions of nature and humans for the sake of the Great Commission, his own personal redemption, and knowledge.

What motivates a person to pursue the Great Commission? What led Daniel Little on his restless pursuit into the wilderness of nature and the mind? Perhaps he wished to conform to Christ's commandment to spread the Word to *all nations*, as recorded in the Gospel of Matthew. Perhaps he believed in bringing the Word to the *whole creation*, hence to all places, even the most sparsely inhabited, as recorded in the Gospel of Mark. Perhaps his personal sense of sin and redemption demanded that he show others a similar way to peace and life. Perhaps it was distant memory, a whistle from the past, an urge to return to a time when he had peace of mind, when he knew little fear, when Evil did not taunt him with the possibility of shattered expectations. To bring Christianity to the original source of fear was the means to expiate it, come to terms with foreboding and end the anguish of the spirit.

2 PASTOR LITTLE

Daniel Little was born in Newburyport, Massachusetts, along the Merrimack River, which flowed from the White Mountains of New Hampshire, draining the waters of south-central New Hampshire and northeastern Massachusetts. His parents Daniel Little, Sr., and Abiah Clement took their large family of seven children, including the infant Daniel, Jr., upriver to Haverhill around the time of his birth in 1724. During his childhood, Daniel lived in the northern part of the town of Haverhill, in a forested region called Timberlane, which, when he was seventeen years old, became the Haverhill District, later Hampstead, New Hampshire.

The region in which Daniel Little, Jr., was born was heavily wooded and well-watered, where farmland, once cleared, was productive and the people could become prosperous in growing crops and raising livestock. Woodlands along river valleys near the sea yielded temperate if humid summers and cold, snowy winters. It was a pastoral, rural, good life, and the people returned thanks to God on the Sabbath in Congregational churches up and down the coast and inland along pure, cold rivers.

The chief concerns of the inhabitants of the Merrimack Valley of Massachusetts and New Hampshire was to farm their lands, seek protection from enemy incursions, and live in as cohesive a way as possible. New England towns were typically very large townships where townspeople could farm hundreds of acres and provide for their sons and daughters. Miles often separated farmers from town centers, where the Congregational church stood. As towns grew, farmers in outlying districts sought by application to the General Court (of Massachusetts or New Hampshire) to form their own parishes in which the community, according to the Congregational way, would choose their own minister and work together to have small commonwealths that operated according to the Protestant Christian way of life. The creation of new parishes rarely occurred without some controversy.

There was provincial controversy as well. Puritans from England settled Massachusetts in the 1600s while landed proprietors and dissenters (from Massachusetts Puritanism) settled New Hampshire at the same time. The disputes between Massachusetts and New Hampshire over their shared boundaries occurred for many years. Ultimately, the two provinces in 1741 agreed mutually upon the eastern and western (and southern) boundaries. The upshot was that some Massachusetts towns had to give up claims to land. Haverhill, founded in 1641 because of the influx of English immigrants coming to Massachusetts seeking to practice Protestant Congregationalism, was one such town. Puritan immigrants in the 1630s and 1640s settled in the northeastern fringes of the province along the Merrimack Valley. A century later, the dispute over the provincial line split the town of Haverhill.

Provincial politics intervened in the lives of the people of Haverhill, forcing some of them to adapt to becoming citizens of New Hampshire. The determination of the provincial line caused quite a controversy among the inhabitants, who now found their parishes divided, and their loyalties to a pastor/church and province upset. There were five Little families that lived north of the line, Daniel Little's family being one of them. Daniel Little, Sr., a tanner, had been a local leader in the Haverhill Timberlane region, and continued, under New Hampshire jurisdiction, as a town moderator, justice of the peace, selectman, and parish deacon.[1]

By the time that these local and provincial political matters were occurring, in the 1740s, Daniel Little, Jr., was a teen-aged boy who was being educated according to the educational standards of the time—in the classics, especially Greek, Latin, and Hebrew. At some point in the 1730s, young Daniel journeyed down the Merrimack to his place of birth, where the Harvard graduate Stephen Sewall tutored Daniel and other children. Sewall was from a well-known Newburyport family. After earning his baccalaureate in 1731, the twenty-three-year old Sewall served as part of the Newbury militia company, and became a tutor in the town's third parish.[2] The elder Little undoubtedly earned a sufficient income to send his son Daniel to Harvard, the most famous seminary in central and northern New England. But according to an early biographer of the younger Daniel, the father eschewed sending his son to "a public seminary of learning," believing that, "though there are greater advantages for proficiency in the knowledge of the liberal arts and sciences at an university, yet there is also greater

---

1 George W. Chase, *The History of Haverhill, Massachusetts, from its first settlement in 1640, to the Year 1860* (Haverhill, MA: By the author, 1861), 310-11, 316. Daniel Little, Sr., in the new town of Hampstead, "by the act of incorporation, . . . was designated as the person to call the first town meeting under the charter."

2 John J. Currier, *History of Newbury, Massachusetts, 1635-1902* (Newbury, MA: Damrell and Upham, 1902), 568, 656.

danger that the principles and morals of youth may be depraved there, by the society, the evil communications and examples, which may there be met with." Rather, the father believed that it was best for his son to live "in a well ordered family, under the eye and government of a pious and prudent tutor."[3]

The small town of Newburyport at the mouth of the Merrimack was not Cambridge, to be sure, yet temptation can surface anywhere, as Daniel Little discovered here, and at other places that he lived in life. Temptation may be manifested in conflict, in disagreement, in the search for knowledge, in feeling the effects of sin—feelings of inadequacy, of not knowing God's will, of not feeling a saving change, in the utter helplessness once feels in confronting the large world. The elder Little had experienced such challenges, and either overtly or subtly had transferred his fears, his anguish, to his son.

The river valleys of the northern New England coast provided the common setting for Daniel Little's life and actions. After his youth living next to and near the Merrimack River, he spent a few years of religious training living along the York River in Maine. As an itinerant pastor, the Piscataqua River and its tributaries were the waters upon which he traveled. Once he settled in Kennebunk, Maine, he lived along the Kennebunk River. As a missionary, he journeyed up the Saco River and spent many years traveling the Penobscot River valley.

During or after his initial education in the rhetorical aspects of the liberal arts, Little (or his father, for him)

---

[3] *Piscataqua Evangelical Magazine*, volume 2, 1806, 42.

expressed a desire to be trained as a gospel minister. To this end, he traveled north across the New Hampshire border into the Massachusetts jurisdiction of Maine, staying with the Rev. Joseph Moody in the town of York. York was like Newburyport, Haverhill, and Hampstead, a pretty little town surrounded by the forest of paper birch, oak, and pine trees. The massive white pine dominated the forest, their long, narrow trunks seemingly piercing the lower atmosphere. The York River, a small river flowing from inland ponds and streams, rushed through the town to the sea. A small harbor between points of land provided safe haven for sailing vessels.

Reconstructing the years in the life of a person who lived 270 years ago has this caveat, that the records for such life are sporadic and haphazard. The records for the early life of Daniel Little are few and far between, being mostly based on tradition handed down and recorded many years afterward in the accounts of local antiquarians. Anecdotes are untrustworthy, but at the same time cannot be out of hand rejected, because, like myth, anecdotal historical traditions have some basis in fact—precisely what is unclear. Different ecclesiastical and local historians have either accepted or rejected the tradition that Daniel Little studied with the Rev. Joseph Moody of York. But Little's character seemed a match for Moody's, so it seems more likely than not—and the story goes like this:

Joseph Moody was born in 1700, and graduated from Harvard in 1718. He was the son of Samuel Moody, a well-respected minister in York. Joseph was studious and precocious, and decided on a public career practicing law. But by the time he was a justice of the Court of Sessions, his father determined that he was wasting his time and God-given talents on secular matters. He put pressure on Joseph to renounce the law and become a minister of the second parish in York. The emotional consequences on Joseph were immense. He felt completely inadequate to represent the Lord of the Universe before his small parish. This inadequacy translated into an overbearing weight of sin upon him. Unable to look his parishioners, or anyone else, in the eye, as if he were looking at God Himself in the eye, Moody veiled his face in public, ate alone, and eventually decided that he could no longer serve as a pastor. "He would visit and frequently pray with the sick, and in private families, and did a few times in public, with great fervency, pertinency, and devotion; but always insisted that he was only the voice of others on these occasions."[4]

Edward Bourne, who wrote *The History of Wells and Kennebunk*, recorded an undated instance the setting for which was York in the years after Little had completed his mentorship with Moody. Little "was a prominent candidate for the pulpit" of Moody's old parish in York, and was preparing a fast day sermon. "Moody, who had taken a deep interest in him, learning that he was to preach that day, took pains to ascertain where he was to lodge; and rising early in the morning, went to the window of his bed-room and cried out: 'Daniel Little! Daniel Little! The birds are up and praising God, and you are here asleep. You have the sins of

---

4 W. Woodford Clayton, *History of York County, Maine* (Philadelphia: Everts & Peck, 1880), 225; Jonathan Greenleaf, *Sketches of the Ecclesiastical History of the State of Maine* (Portsmouth, NH: Harrison Gray, 1821), 13; Charles E. Banks, *History of York, Maine* vol. 2 (Boston: 1931, 1935; reprint Baltimore. Regional Publishing Co., 1967), 80-83.

a whole nation to confess to-day and yet are asleep'."

Encompassed in this one anecdote are the two expressions of Christ's Great Commission, as expressed by Matthew (to spread the word to the nations) and Mark (to spread the word to the whole creation). Little's immediate responsibility was to the humans of this parish in York, who represented the humans of the British empire, and indeed of the whole world. But who had arisen before God's messenger but the birds themselves, praising God earlier, and more effectively, than Daniel Little ever could have. Henceforth, according to Bourne, Little arose with the birds to spread the glory of God, a messenger singing in harmony with the creation.[5]

Little, who after his mentorship with Moody was ordained by "associated ministers of the county of York," did not become a pastor in York.[6] He served, rather, as an itinerant in different northern New England parishes until he settled down in Kennebunk. In 1747, Little served for a time at the North Church at Portsmouth, New Hampshire—a beautiful congregational church situated in Market Square just south of the Piscataqua River. But he did not receive a call from that parish. He kept school for a time in Wells (later Kennebunk), Maine, filling in at Berwick and York, then preached in Brentwood, New Hampshire. Brentwood was a town north of Hampstead and Haverhill in a forested region on the Squamscott River. For several years the town had been in conflict over religious worship, as the parishes of

---

5 Edward E. Bourne, *The History of Wells and Kennebunk* (Portland, ME: B. Thurston & Co., 1875), 708.

6 *Piscataqua Evangelical Magazine*, 42.

other towns, such as Exeter and Kingston, were too far to travel to, especially in winter. But Brentwood, divided by the river, was also divided by townspeople who wanted the meetinghouse to be on their side of the river (north or south). For a time a meetinghouse was built at Keeneborough, though half the town refused to attend. These people, south of the river, worked to build their own meetinghouse, and hired itinerant preachers to minister to their needs in the meantime. The controversy continued throughout the 1740s. Daniel Little preached for a year and a half at Brentwood in 1748 and 1749. He found himself caught in the middle of the conflict as townspeople argued against other townspeople over their church and future salvation. Little's mild-mannered, humble approach to people endeared him to the parishioners, who decided to call him to the job of being their permanent pastor. He responded: "I have taken the advice of ministers and particular friends who know your case, and have weighed the affair, I hope, without partiality; and upon the clearest view, the difficulties you meet with at present, and the prospect of greater hereafter by reason of your perplext and uncertain circumstances as a Parish, oblige me to manifest my answer to your call in the negative. You have my prayers that your difficulties may be removed, and that the God of love and peace may be with you and bless you."[7] In life, Daniel Little exhibited patience when it came to the affairs of God; he was willing to wait to answer the summons that he believed was the true calling.

He did not wait long. Within eight months he was

---

7 Benjamin A. Dean, *Annals of the Brentwood, N. H. Congregational Church and Parish* (Boston: T. W. Ripley, 1889), 11-12.

preaching full time at the second parish of Wells, Maine, in what would become the town of Kennebunk. The people of Wells, a seacoast township north of York and south of the Kennebunk River, experienced the same difficulties of other New England towns: one meetinghouse and a large community of people, some of whom lived miles away. Those who lived in the northern part of Wells, between the Mousam and Kennebunk rivers, determined to have their own parish and meetinghouse during the 1740s. The town leaders of Wells were against the project, but the resourceful people of what became Kennebunk built the meetinghouse anyway. The Massachusetts General Court supported the outlivers, and the Second Parish of Wells (First Parish of Kennebunk) was founded in June, 1750.[8]

    Daniel Little, already known from his time as a teacher in Wells, received the call from the Second Parish in August. The parish offered the pastor a salary, a 100£ one-time payment, and firewood. Little requested that the 100£ be used to purchase land upon which he would build his home. After lengthy negotiations, and even lengthier deliberation by the young pastor, Little eventually wrote the parish a letter at the end of January, 1751, that he had "the satisfaction . . . in observing the many signal tokens of the wise conduct and the various blessings of Divine Providence vouchsafed towards you as a people . . . , particularly in the appearance of so happy a degree of charity and brotherly love, and especially the continuance of such a temper and disposition manifested by your late conduct and entire unanimity." The unity of the parish indicated to Little the

---

8 Bourne, *History of Wells and Kennebunk*, 392-394.

willingness of the people to join him "with a view to the honor of Christ, humbly relying upon the conduct and assistance of the Divine Spirit." Little, knowing and fearing the task, "being sensible of my many imperfections, and great unequalness to a work so sacred and important as the gospel ministry," agreed to accept their offer.[9]

Rev. Little took charge of the flock in March, 1751. The church building was a still under construction, having been undauntingly built by the contributions and labor of all involved during the previous two years. Officers and deacons were appointed, plate purchased for communion, and pastor and parishioners signed the church covenant. The covenant was typical of eighteenth-century congregationalism: the parishioners professed their belief in the Holy Trinity, agreed upon the mutual support they must give to one-another, and promised to raise their children in Christ. Two months later, pastor and parishioners signed a baptismal covenant as well as a communion covenant, baptism and communion being the two chief sacraments of congregational churches. The parishioners included infants in "the Gospel Covenant" and pledged to bring up children to serve God in "paths of holy obedience.[10]

Early American pastors sought to achieve as much harmony as possible in their parishes—this was clearly Daniel Little's goal, generally (if church records and anecdotal accounts are sufficient evidence) achieved. He

---

9 Ibid., 395-396; *Records of the First Parish Church of Kennebunk: including Records of Baptisms, Marriages, and Deaths, 1750-1890*, Maine Historical Society.

10 Bourne, *History of Wells and Kennebunk*, 393, 396-399; *Records of the First Parish Church*.

sought in his meetings with parishioners that the light of mutual understanding would be shed among them. But humans fall short. One of the most common sins was fornication—breaking the Seventh Commandment—which, upon confessing before the congregation, would be forgiven and mutual communion of sinner and congregation restored. In time Rev. Little allowed fornicators to confess privately rather than before the whole congregation. He was not one to bring hell-fire and damnation before a person or people, either privately or in sermons, rather to encourage mutual love, reflecting the love of Christ. If people were not attending meeting, Little met with them to discuss the causes and encourage their return. Most of his duties, besides preparing sermons and visiting the sick, involving administering the traditional church sacrament of baptism, and recording the event in the parish records. He encouraged charitableness in his parish, such that every Sabbath the basket was passed about and coins accumulated to present to some needy person or community. In 1770, after Marblehead, on the Massachusetts coast near Cape Anne, suffered from devastating storms, the Kennebunk parish donated funds for their relief.[11]

Cohesion and harmony in family life was likewise of utmost importance to a congregational minister. Lacking informal, private records of Little's family, we have little to go on, save the records of the Kennebunk parish of baptism and communion, and the anecdotes of friends. Daniel and Mary Emerson of Malden, Massachusetts, were married on December 5, 1751. She was the daughter of Joseph Emerson,

---

11 Bourne, *History of Wells and Kennebunk*, 399.

Harvard graduate and great-grandfather of Ralph Waldo Emerson. An early eulogist said of Mary, "She was a pious and ingenious gentlewomen." Their marriage lasted for seven and one-half years; she died in childbirth bearing their third child, Daniel. Previously, Daniel and Mary had Joseph, born in October, 1752, and Mary, born June, 1756. Of these three children, the first, Joseph, died in infancy, as did the third, Daniel. The burden of death could challenge the patience as well as the credulity of the most devout Christian. To bury two infants, two wonderful examples of God's grace, each a singular incarnation, took a significant toll on Daniel, who doubtlessly submerged his feelings under the weight of philosophy and faith. What more proof is needed to show humans to be doomed to mirror the passing instant, overwhelmed by the passage of time, uncertain where they are going and where they have been, living only in the narcissistic moment?[12]

Daniel waited about a year and a half to remarry. She was Sarah Coffin from Newburyport, who, according to a friend, was "a pious and agreeable companion." Sarah brother's Paul was Little's friend and brother minister at Buxton, Maine. Daniel and Sarah "lived together as heirs of the grace of life, and helpers of each other's joy, more than forty-two years." The parish records for December 16, 1759, record that "Sarah, the wife of the Revd. Mr. Little, received to full communion." Soon they had children: Nathaniel Coffin, baptized August 8, 1762; Sarah, baptized February 12, 1764;

---

12 *Records of the First Parish Church*; *Piscataqua Evangelical Magazine*, 82; Clifford K. Shipton, *Biographical Sketches of Those Who Attended Harvard College* (Sibley's Harvard Graduates) Volume 12 (Boston, Massachusetts Historical Society, 1962), 47.

Margaret, baptized March 30, 1765; David, baptized December 7, 1766; Hannah, baptized June 10, 1770. Two others were apparently not included in the parish records. Of these seven, only three survived Daniel and Sarah.[13]

Death, as it were, was a frequent visitor to the Little household, intervening in their quietude, in their harmony, in their faith and hope. Daniel and Sarah Little were well known among the members of the Northern New England religious community, such as in and about the Piscataqua River valley. The Piscataqua Missionary Society, which published the short-lived *Piscataqua Evangelical Magazine*, wrote a posthumous account of Daniel Little, clearly based on the formal familiarity of the times. The unnamed author, who knew Little intimately, described him as showing "great respect, kindness and politeness," toward his wives, and "mildness and tenderness" toward his children. Little disagreed with the typical mode of parenting at the time, "that austere method of conduct, which some think is necessary in the head of a family to keep up authority and maintain government." Daniel Little "endeavoured to render himself agreeable to them, and engage their love; and thought that in this way it was more easy to bend their minds to due subjection, than by keeping them at an awful distance; that much familiarity prudently used would not breed contempt; and that an admonition given with softness would often sink deeper, and be more effectual, than when clothed with an austere frown." The father resolved that his family should "serve the Lord . . . by a very strict and serious

---

[13] *Records of the First Parish Church*; *Piscataqua Evangelical Magazine*, 82; Shipton, *Biographical Sketches*, 47.

observance of the duties and exercises of religious worship every day. The scriptures were read morning and evening with practical observations and devout prayers and thanksgivings." The author of the account, having been with the Littles on the Sabbath, recalled "the very solemn, earnest and affectionate manner in which he . . . addressed his children, exhorting and charging them not to neglect the care of their souls' salvation, but turn to God without delay with all their hearts; and of the fervent and pathetic prayers, which he has put up for them for the blessings of divine grace."[14]

Death disturbed the household, but not poverty. Daniel and Sarah were frugal without being parsimonious, so that the family always had what they needed, with a bit of comfort besides. Although his salary as a gospel minister was slight, especially during times of conflict, "Mr. Little, not despising the day of small things, and trusting in the promise, that to those, who seek first the kingdom of God and his righteousness, all things needful shall be added," embraced his role as a small-town pastor. Daniel Little also lacked the presumptuousness so characteristic of his time, especially among Protestant ministers, in assuming that great thoughts might bring light to God's mysteries. Rather, "deep speculations on abstruse points, analyzing and unravelling the cunningly woven cobwebs of metaphysical sophistry, were not agreeable to his genius or taste." Little lived "an active" rather "than contemplative life." "If some others might be more fit to meet and speak with the enemy in the gate, he was well qualified and disposed to plant, and

---

14 *Piscataqua Evangelical Magazine*, 82-83. See also Jonathan E. Helmreich, *Eternal Hope: The Life of Timothy Alden, Jr.* (Cranbury, NJ: Cornwall Books, 2001).

water, and dress the vine in the vineyard of the Lord." Little was filled with physical and psychical energy: "His thoughts sprung and flowed with great quickness; and it was his own observation of himself, that his first thoughts were best; that they were not ordinarily ripened and improved, but rather perplexed, by pondering and deliberation." He worked quickly, accomplished his goals expediently. His prayers tended to be extemporaneous, and he prayed with such "facility" and with a "devout heart," that he appeared, in prayer, to be "inspired from above in an unusual manner." He did not keep to himself in the parsonage, but often went door to door, seeking the outcast, consoling the hurting, blessing the plentiful. His sermons were practical, filled with good advice rather than theological strictures. He believed not in splitting hairs but grooming his parishioners with the great truths of love, peace, faith, and hope. He was not typically eloquent, but his words appeared truthful. He embraced other religious views in an ecumenical fashion, believing in charitableness rather than ferocious debate. He was not keen to follow the great debates of the New Lights and Old Lights, so popular at the time, but to steer a middle ground, focusing on the obvious truths of the Scripture and God.[15]

The unnamed writer of the *Strictures of the Life, &c. of the Rev. Daniel Little* had been a friend and companion. He knew Little to have been "cheerful and sociable," uniting in one character "the politeness and urbanity of the gentleman, the familiarity and kindness of the friend, and the serious piety of the Christian": he was "an agreeable, amiable,

---

15 Ibid., 44-46.

entertaining, and instructive companion." He spent much time visiting his parishioners, such visits designed "to engage love, and invite to a reciprocal freedom of discourse, than to command reverence." He "was free, familiar, and even facetious," though not a jokester, and he enjoyed speaking good of people, even when they were absent; he disliked talking behind a person's back. "He was a rare example of one of great sensibility, and an ardent spirit, who seemed to have no gall in his constitution. The warmth of his temper was all mild, kind, and benevolent. It was said by one, who had been much conversant with him for more than forty years, that he never saw his temper ruffled with anger."[16]

---

16 Ibid., 46-47.

3 EXPLORER ON A MISSION

The large frigate was becalmed in the water just beyond the mouth of the Piscataqua River. The easterlies, essential to propel the vessel against the rushing waters spilling into the Atlantic, were still, and the captain and crew waited. To the southeast lay the Isles of Shoals, barely rising above the waves; northwest was Gerrish Island on the coast of Maine; south of that, across the broad mouth of the Piscataqua River, lay Great Island, and the town of Newcastle. Upriver on the northern shores was the town of Kittery; on the southern shores, the city of Portsmouth. Aboard the frigate were one hundred men waiting for the breeze to stir, to carry the three-masted vessel into the mouth of the river. The men were part of a troop raised by Colonel Jedidiah Preble of Falmouth, who had received a commission from Governor Pownall in March, 1758, to raise a force to participate in the invasion of Canada. Preble and his men were gathering at Kittery under the command of William Pepperrell to wage war against the French and their Indian allies. The year was 1758. The last of the great wars of empire in North America, the French-Indian War, was in its fourth year.

From the beginning of European voyages along coastal Maine the incredible bounty of Maine attracted admiration and plans for settlements to exploit the virgin wilderness. French and English colonists discovered what the Indians had long known, that Maine could supply its inhabitants' material needs--and much more. Different peoples of different political and cultural backgrounds struggled to control such a fertile area. Indeed, even before the coming of the English and French the Indian tribes of the region fought for control of Maine's resources. In the wake of the voyages of the Frenchman Samuel de Champlain and the Englishman Martin Pring, the French and English sought to assert their self-proclaimed rights to govern the land and exploit its riches. The French tended to stay in the easternmost parts, the Penobscot, St. Croix, and St. John's river valleys; the English focused on the Piscataqua, Saco, and Kennebec. Inevitably, of course, competition would bring the adventurous and ambitious to cross the supposed boundaries that separated one side from the other. Besides, French and English competition over Maine was in microcosm what was occurring throughout North America, as the French tried to extend their power from New France and the St. Lawrence River valley south to the Great Lakes and Ohio, Mississippi, and Missouri river valleys, and the English sought to maintain their vital interest of the thirteen colonies and at the same time expand further inland in search of land and resources. Conflict over territory inevitably erupted: hence began the Indian Wars that plagued Maine for almost a century.

The many Algonquian Indian tribes of Maine, including the Abenaki, Passamaquoddy, Penobscot, Penacook, Piscataqua, Sokokis, Micmac, Pequod, Pequawket, and Norridgewock, had been involved in conflict and battle among themselves for generations. When the English and French arrived in the sixteenth and seventeenth centuries, Indian tribes became embroiled in the European contests for control of North America. The French, especially because of missionaries of the Franciscan and Jesuit orders, came to know the Algonquians, lived with them, converted them.

The Protestant Anglicans were not as apt to live among the tribes, and were viewed with more suspicion by the Algonquians. The French used their close relationship with their allied Catholic converts to raid English settlements in northern New England throughout almost a century of war, from the 1670s and King Philip's War, through the 1680s and 1690s and King William's War, then Queen Anne's War in the early eighteenth century, followed by Dummer's War in the 1720s, then King George's War in the 1740s, and finally the French-Indian War from 1755-1763.

During the French-Indian War, the English had determined that the best offense against the French was an attack on their holdings north of Maine in Acadia and Quebec. Massachusetts governor Thomas Pownall and William Pepperrell planned to launch attacks from Lake George on French holdings on and north of Lake Champlain, as well as an attack on Louisburg, the French fortress situated at the southeastern corner of Cape Breton Island.

After waiting off shore on May 22nd, the winds stirred on the 23rd, allowing the ships to enter the river and make port at Kittery. There, Preble's recruits listened to a sermon by Rev. John Rogers, and swore to abide by the King and the Governor and their commanders on this treacherous enterprise. The men prepared to depart on May 27th. Their chaplain, the Rev. Daniel Little, had not yet arrived. Little, two months before, although his wife Mary was with child, had volunteered to serve as chaplain to the Maine troops. By the time the three frigates under Preble's command, each with one hundred men, sailed from Falmouth for Kittery on May 21st, Mary was nearing the end of the pregnancy, which added to the anticipation and anxiety that Daniel already felt about being gone so long on a journey by sea and land into Quebec. On the 23rd, Mary gave birth to a son; she was "comfortable, and in the highest joy" when Daniel departed for a brief excursion, where is not known--doubtless in preparation for his journey south to Kittery to join the troops. Notwithstanding the birth, "everything we tho't look[ed] most Smiling upon my proposed Absence from my Family." Daniel and Mary lived in a two-story clapboard house near Kennebunk Landing, where the river met the road and ships loaded and unloaded cargo. Approaching home on the 24th, he met a "messenger in the greatest Haste informing [me] that my Wife was at the point of Death." "Alas, I am now in the Depths of Sorrow. My Wife was seized yesterday Morning with the most Shocking Fits and ever Since deprived of Reason and Speech."[17]

The mother of two young children and a newborn child, Mary Little, survived the child's birth only one week. Daniel baptized the boy, christened Daniel, the same day, June 2nd, that Mary died. The child survived the mother only nine days, dying on June 11th. About these melancholy events, the historical record is largely silent regarding Daniel Little's anguish. We can only imagine.

Little penned a brief note to William Pepperrell on May 25th. "I tho't it my Duty to inform your Hon[our] as Soon as possible that I am oblig'd in duty to resign my Place as Chaplain to Coll. Preble's Regiment." The ways of God are inscrutable. Why should a Gospel minister serving the Lord

---

17 George H. Preble, *Genealogical Sketch of the First Three Generations of Prebles in America* (Boston: David Clapp, 1868), 48; Hugh E. McLellan, *History of Gorham, Maine* (Portland, ME: Smith & Sale, 1903), 66; Daniel Little to Sir William Pepperrell, May 25, 1758, Rauner Library, Dartmouth College.

be exempt from God's will? "It may be necessary to observe in Hon[our] to Divine Providence that none of my People, who know the State of my Family thinks that the present affliction was occasioned by my Designed Absence." This was, of course, a possibility. That her husband was preparing to depart for who knows how long on a dangerous journey in wartime to Quebec at the same time that she was giving birth—this was a heavy, even intolerable, burden. "My Wife was in the most Christian manner resign'd," he wrote to Pepperrell, telling himself the same thing, "so that this afflicting Providence to me can be of no discouragement to any of my Brethren to take my Place."[18]

Was Little implying in his letter to Pepperrell that God looked down upon his determination to join troops in war against other Christians, albeit Catholic Christians, in Canada? Unexpected death during the same time, during these years of war against the French and their Indian allies, that Little had heard the sound of the war whistle, seems to have combined to urge him to devote himself for the sake of

---

18 Little to Pepperrell, 5/25/1758. The incidents surrounding Little's chaplaincy, resignation, and return home are vague and the secondary sources inaccurate. The *Register of the Officers and Members of the Society of Colonial Wars in the State of Maine* (Portland: Marks Printing House, 1905), 120, states that "it was while he was with Preble's regiment at Lake George, that his first wife died. . . . These afflictions led him to resign his chaplaincy, and he returned home." The regiment did not, however, depart Kittery until May 27th, and Little was home in Kennebunk—so he clearly never went to Lake George. According to *Historical Collections of the Essex Institute*, "The Journal of the Rev. John Cleaveland," 12(1874): 92-94: John Cleaveland's brother Ebenezer Cleaveland was to go as Colonel Preble's chaplain: Preble wrote to Pepperrell to that effect on June 14th, "for a warrant for brother, in case Mr. Little should conclude absolutely not to come." Little was not with them in New York, nor did he ever go.

the Great Commission. Little remarried and continued his ministry in Kennebunk, all the while inspired to follow in the wake of other messengers of the Gospel, bringing the *word* to those who had never heard it, those who had heard it but incorrectly, and those who had heard it but ignored it.

The experiences and feelings of Daniel Little were akin to the Apostle Paul, the first missionary, whose work was in response to the burden of sin. Paul was plagued with an "angel of Satan," guilt and the continual need for atonement, which kept him dependent upon God's grace, and compelled him to tell others, to replay his own experience over and over, so in a way to reassure himself that he was indeed redeemed.

The experiences of Paul, the psychology of the missionary, are found throughout time, found centuries later in North America among Protestants such as Daniel Little who were looking for more, were trying to make sense of the *message* that they were themselves bringing to others. The *messengers* to the American Indians were weak, uncertain, and sinful, engaged in a personal journey in the wilderness among unknown peoples, a journey of redemption and atonement. There is already mystery and uncertainty in confronting the everyday, in confronting the newness of experience inherent in the passage of time. But to embrace even further change and uncertainty by exploration into the unknown, bringing the message to others, is to increase anxiety, hence to increase reliance upon God.

Missionaries, in spreading the Gospel, were doing so in part as a response to their own sin, the awareness of which led them to act. There was a restless energy felt by missionaries to expiate and atone for their own transgressions, the weight of human existence, by trying to remove those of others. They were trying to remove the splinter from the eyes of others notwithstanding the huge plank in their own. Daily the weight of personal sin required movement; the air of the wilderness helped the missionary not to suffocate. What else drives a person to do this but atonement? Like Paul reaching out to the Gentiles, American Protestant missionaries reached out to Indians, humans believed to be in a pre-redeemed state, when sin is rampant and before humans have been saved by Christ, when Satan holds sway—a time and state that can recur again and again when temptation brings a person back to an earlier, pre-redeemed state. This id-like part of us, the savage part, is ubiquitous, and if one is not constantly vigilant it will recur. Missionary work is vigilance for one's own continual redemption.

The origins of Indians fascinated seventeenth and eighteenth-century missionaries because discoverers and colonists of America had been confronted with the presence of a people who were un-touched by the Great Commission. Missionaries had traveled to most countries of the world by the time of Columbus's voyage, and it was obvious that even those places touched by the Great Commission could easily return to sin. But what about a people never so touched? It is similar to thinking about oneself before and after any great event of education or civilization or conversion. What was humanity like before then after the Incarnation? American Protestant missionaries were as a result historians of the peculiar experience of America: they were fascinated by the past, both distant and not so distant; and by personal history, that is, their own psychology.

The psychology of the missionary involves the elevated sense of self. How does God appoint a person to be a messenger? For a person to assume such a role is an indication of a measure of self-importance, some hint of self-perceived greatness. Spiritual experience has convinced such a person to engage in an arduous, sometimes dangerous role. A sense of selection, or election, which involves a spiritual or mystical experience, exists. What is this but a calling, and what is a calling but a mystical experience—a communication with the divine? This self-knowledge, of limitations and possibilities, propels and harbors the messenger going forth in strange lands among strange peoples. Missionaries such as Daniel Little possessed an intuitive strength gained through prayer and religious struggle to know what and who is God and how one relates to God, faith in God's will, and the continual battle waged against sin and the humility consequent thereon.

There had been many missionaries—ordained and self-appointed, ad hoc—in North America during the previous several centuries. Few had penetrated the forested and mountainous extremes of Maine. Some of Daniel Little's Maine colleagues engaged in modest missionary activities, such as Little's neighbor, friend, brother-in-law and fellow laborer in God's vineyard, Rev. Paul Coffin, who lived at Buxton, north of Kennebunk near the Saco River. Little had participated in the ordination of Paul Coffin during the winter of 1763. The town of Buxton was then known as Narraganset No. 1. Little set out with Rev. Moses Hemmenway of Wells to make the journey of twenty miles to Buxton. Snow was deep, and the men had to wear snowshoes. They became lost in the snowstorm, but found their way to the frozen Saco River, where they bivouacked for the night, desperately cold, in danger of freezing. With dawn, they were able to find their way to Buxton, arriving at the meetinghouse about the time of the scheduled ordination.[19]

Five years later, Rev. Paul Coffin, settled in Buxton, determined to travel northwest to the upper Saco valley and the town of Fryeburg. Such frontier pastors often made it a point to travel to outlying regions where white settlers did not have the advantage of a settled religious community. Such frontier towns as Fryeburg rarely enjoyed the presence of a pastor to baptize children, celebrate communion, catechize the inhabitants, and preach from the Gospel.

It was to these manifold ends of sharing the Christian sacraments that Daniel Little decided during the 1770s to become a messenger for Christ to people who rarely, or had never, heard it. A few years after his death in 1801 a friend and fellow laborer recalled that "the state of those plantations in the eastern parts of the District of Maine, which had not the word of God and ordinances of the gospel regularly dispensed among them, and so were in danger of losing the impressions of religion and morality, lay heavy on his mind." Why Daniel Little should feel the burden of responsibility for such people is never explicitly stated or confessed—by himself or others—except for suggestions in his journals that the sufferings he had undergone, and the solace he had received from Christ, made him empathetically aware that others besides himself who

---

19 The story of Little's journey to Buxton is told by Bourne, *History of Wells and Kennebunk*, 719.

suffered required such solace—and who was to give it to them if not him?[20]

He received encouragement in these endeavors from local and regional associations of ministers. New England congregational ministers regularly shared the pulpit with one-another for purposes of illness or travel. There were several associations of ministers in New Hampshire and Maine in which Little participated. The Eastern Association of Ministers had been formed in the 1740s, and joined together clergymen of the eastern shores and inland lands north of Boston. Little was a member of an association of ministers of the County of York, of which Wells was a part. Little's interests in the Great Commission was known to members of this association, which resulted, in 1772, in an appointment as "Missionary to the Eastern Settlements" by a group of Trustees, recognized by the Massachusetts General Court, devoted to Eastern Missions. Many years later Little described the events in a letter to Samuel Phillips: "In the Year 1772 at a Meeting of the associated Ministers in the County of York, they took into consideration the particular State of those Plantations with respect to the Means of religious instruction, especially the Settlements on the river and Bay of Penobscot, and unanimously agreed to petition the Gen[eral] Court [of Massachusetts] for a Grant for the Support of a Missionary among them (there being not then one settled Minister thro' so large extent of that part of the Country). The Gen[era]l Court in their Wisdom and goodness immediately upon receiving the petition, made a grant Sufficient for the Support of a Missionary, during a

---

20 *Piscataqua Evangelical Magazine*, 85.

part of 5 Summers, and appointed a Committee for the Choice and direction of the same, Viz. the Rev[ere]d Dr. Stevns of Kittery, the rev'd Messrs. Lyman and Lankton of York. And in the Same year of the grant, by the direction of said Committee, I gave an opening to the Mission."[21]

The French-Indian War had a profound impact on Daniel Little and the people of Maine. Upon the surrender of France, and the removal, for good, of the French and Indian threat along the primary rivers of Maine, the people of Massachusetts, New Hampshire, and Maine began to envision possibilities for settling the rich lands of the eastern frontier. The Massachusetts General Court systematized the settlement of the Maine frontier with land grants to, especially, veterans of the French-Indian War who were willing to bring and sponsor people to clear and farm the acreage of the grant. Beginning in 1762, veteran officers brought their families, friends, and associates to the eastern frontier. The Penobscot bay and valley, once a dangerous place because it was a central gathering place for the French and their Abenaki allies, now free of threat, with Fort Pownall signifying British-American control, became a destination for people such as Colonel Jonathan Buck, Joseph Gross, Charles Hutchings, Aaron Banks, Joseph

---

21 R. Pierce Beaver, ed., *American Missions in Bicentennial Perspective* (South Pasadena, CA: American Society of Missiology, 1977), 11; George B. Spalding, *Historical Discourse Delivered on the One Hundredth Anniversary of the Piscataqua Association of Ministers* (Dover, NH: Morning Star Job Printing Office, 1882), 12, 18; Charles L Chaney, *The Birth of Missions in America* (Eugene, OR: Wipf & Stock, 2012), 128; Daniel Little, "General Account of the Rise and Progress of the Eastern Mission By Letter to Honourable Samuel Phillips, Esq.", February 18, 1788, Miscellaneous Bound Manuscripts, Massachusetts Historical Society (hereafter, MHS).

Wood, and Colonel Nathan Parker. During the ensuing decade there were itinerant preachers, often with more stamina and strength than sense and subtlety, who served these scattered peoples east of the Kennebec River. No one of the stature of the Reverend Daniel Little—an ordained Congregational minister, holder of the Master's degree from Harvard, and mature Christian thinker—journeyed into these parts until 1772, when Daniel Little himself ventured forth.

Daniel Little was a sporadic diarist, meaning that he infrequently took the time and put forth the energy to record his motions and thoughts. On his first journey to the Penobscot region in 1772, if he kept a diary, it is lost, so that all that we can say about this journey is through speculation, anecdote, and occasional historical references. How he journeyed from Kennebunk to the Penobscot is unknown, though there were but two possible routes, by land and sea. Two years later, in 1774, he journeyed by sea to Penobscot and returned by land to Kennebunk. Perhaps this was a routine established during his first journey. Little was not given much to the sea. He was hardly a landlubber, but if he had a choice as to how to travel, he would be more apt to choose horseback over coastal schooner. The problem was, that very few people owned horses on the eastern frontier. They traveled by foot, canoe, skiff, or a larger boat with sails. Little probably set forth in July or August and returned at the end of October before the snows came. The only date that we can be sure of is that of October 7, 1772, when he organized a parish at Blue Hill in the Penobscot region. On his journey in 1774, his journal entries imply familiarity with many of the places that he visited. Indeed, in his 1788 letter to Samuel Phillips, Little wrote that "I visited all the plantations from Belfast, on the western side of the Bay of Penobscot, eastward as far as Narraquagus" River or Bay.[22] We can assume, therefore, that the journey of 1772 was very much like that of 1774. Hence, we will allow the travels of adventures of Daniel Little from July to October, 1774, as representing as well his journey of two years before.

"July 1. The Trustees for the Eastern Mission having applied to me for 3 or 4 months service in the new settlement on the Eastern shore of this Province, and my people having consented to the same, took leave of my dear family, & rode to Winter Harbour in Saco for a passage having been informed of a vessel then bound to Union River."[23] Winter Harbour, now the town of Biddeford, was on the southern shores of the Saco River across from Pepperellborough, now the town of Saco. Winter Harbour was about ten miles away, a couple of hours by horse. Once Little arrived, he stayed "at Mr. Merrill's," perhaps a local taverner serving travelers. The vessel rode at anchor, awaiting the dawn. The captain was taking "a freight of cattle," fifteen head, to the Penobscot. Little and ten others boarded as passengers, and they set forth down the river at sunset, when the tide was

---

22 Little, "General Account of the Rise and Progress of the Eastern Mission."

23 All of Daniel Little's extant journals are found at the Brick Store Museum, Kennebunk, Maine. At some point in the past, an unidentified Museum staff member typed the manuscripts from the originals, which apparently no longer exist. These typed transcriptions have some typographical errors, such as misspellings, but appear to be otherwise accurate, hence are the best source by which to retrace Little's journeys. The several journals are combined together into one manuscript, and paginated, not entirely by chronological occurrence. Little's 1774 journal, titled "Mr. Little's Journal from July 1 1774 to October 10, 1774" will be designated herein as *Journal*, 1774, with page numbers referring to the typed manuscript. All subsequent journals will be so noted.

high, passing over a shallow sand bar at the river's mouth. Little, ever the pastor, prayed with "the company," perhaps crew as well as passengers, before retiring. They sailed northeast across Saco Bay to Cape Elizabeth, which they passed to port, continuing across Casco Bay toward the mouth of the Kennebec, which they kept to port continuing east-northeast through the night. Little slept, or tried to sleep, during this night passage. At dawn they found themselves at the entrance of Penobscot Bay. Little's journey does not indicate the location, but perhaps near Vinalhaven or Owl's Head. They were becalmed, awaiting a following wind to head into the bay. During the day of July 3rd, the Sabbath, aboard ship, Little was very ill, perhaps sea sick, and could not "perform any divine service." Nevertheless, the pastor "sent up to the people on deck a number of practical books, desired them to read and sing psalms; which they took kindly." It rained all night, but "the storm abated" in the morning, taking with it Little's illness. They could spy the "Penobscot Mountains"—probably the hills about Camden—as the captain and crew tried to negotiate strong head winds driving from the Isle au Haut. If the day was sunny, the water appeared a blue-green; on still days the tall pines covering the islands were reflected, a mirror, in the sea. Near the shore the rocky granite rocks and interstices featured shrubs and ferns; the cries of seagulls were all about; cormorants dove in the waters off shore. The wooden boat, dwarfed by the grandness of the bay, negotiated the many isles between Swans Island and Deer Isle to come to anchor off Naskeag Point. Here Little took the opportunity of being rowed ashore to visit a "Mrs. Watson, formerly one of my neighbours," who he undoubtedly had seen two years before in 1772. "She has been in melancholy condition for a great while, is now forceably confined her room, does not know her own husband or any of the domesticks from strangers—a woman formerly of exemplary virtue, now useless otherwise than for the exercise of some of the most Christian virtues by those who without weariness or complaint take the charge of her."[24]

Returned to the anchored ship, Little and the other passengers spent the night aboard off Naskeag Point. This day, July 5, they cruised uncertainly for eight hours through the Mount Desert Narrows, surrounded by islands and hills, sailing north toward the mouth of Union River. Little had been here during his first visit, and he was glad to reunite with acquaintances formed two years before. Benjamin Joy, who had been on board the ship from Saco, guided Little to his lodgings at Justice Jordan's. The next day was stormy, which elicited the comment: "Happy for us that so many passengers & cumbersome cargo 15 head of cattle, etc. arrived yesterday."[25]

Word spread that Pastor Little had arrived. After resting several days, Little set off to visit the families of Union River. The river, flowing from north to south, was initially a broad tidal river that narrowed into a delightful small, cold stream. Little did not record his means of conveyance, though it was doubtless one of the many birch bark canoes used by the locals since long before the English arrived. These were sturdy, buoyant river craft made from the bark of the paper birch tree, so ubiquitous in Maine. Little

---

24 *Journal*, 1774, 23

25 Ibid, 24.

counseled people about making "a public profession of their religion," and gave a lecture at the home of Captain Benjamin Millikin, the inaugural settler of Union, who had lived in the area since 1767. He and others of the first grantees were charged with settling Protestant families and building sawmills. At Little's lecture, "the people [were] attentive to the word." The following day, a Saturday, Little crossed to the east side of the river, and visited Mr. Joy, his new acquaintance from the voyage. He exhorted those whom he met that it was proper to keep the Sabbath, and he invited them to "Capt. Millican's Barn" on the west side of the river for the "Lord's day" service. He presided over a good congregation, nine of whom professed their faith, and fifteen were baptized. In the afternoon, he went by boat upriver to Patten Bay, near modern Surry, where he visited Captain Patten and his family. The next morning he proceeded east across the bay to Weymouth Point, were Mr. Weymouth was "in great distress of body and mind on the borders of eternity. ... He received instructions" from the pastor "with understanding and good temper." Both Captain Patten and Mr. Weymouth were original settlers of the grants in the wake of the French-Indian War. Little "baptized 4 children and one adult" among a "large company from Union river." Proceeding downriver, he came to Mr. Joy's, his makeshift abode, from whom he learned about the history of this area. The town and river of Union were so-called because originally there were twelve lots for townships on both sides of the river, granted by the government of Massachusetts. There were some disputes over the twelve lots, which upon compromise, was commemorated by the name Union. Little learned that there were at present sixty families, "a very industrious labourious people." The people of the twelve lots of Union were desirous of hearing the word, and had often hired temporary preachers, but had failed in attracting a pastor to settle among them.[26]

Little had an interesting experience on Tuesday, July 12. The day was stormy, forcing him to stay with Benjamin Joy. Several Penobscot Indians visited. They had converted to Catholicism because of French influence with predictable results—at least in Little's mind, who like most New England Protestants despised the teachings of the Roman Catholic church and looked upon their missionary work among the Indians as ineffective. "Rum is their God," Little said of the Indians. "The uncouth, ugly dress, paintings, jargon and singing gave a droll novel entertainment to me." Their Christianity was superficial, he thought; they made the sign of the cross upon themselves and their children repeatedly without knowing why; the sacrament of baptism seemed to have little meaning to them; they were superstitious and believed in magic, thinking that Little, like their Catholic priests of old, could conjure up miracles. This was, perhaps, the first time that Daniel Little came face to face with the people with whom he would spend years interacting and negotiating with—and ministering to.[27]

The next morning Little was off with two guides, "pilots," who led him on a six-mile hike through the woods from Union River east "to the head of Skillings River." There remained a French influence in the area, named for

---

26 Ibid., 24-25; George J. Varney, *Gazetteer of the State of Maine* (Boston: B. B. Russell, 1881), 221, 533

27 *Journal*, 1774, 25-26.

one Lamoine. Six families gathered together for a service and baptism. One of the first English settlers, Thomas McFarland, was present. Thereupon, Little went by river craft south four miles to Swedeland, where he baptized and prayed with the locals. He stayed with Captain Agreen Crabtree, also an early settler. On the 14th he held religious services, blessing people's profession of religion and baptizing youngsters. From here he went by yacht south into Frenchman's Bay, to a place that Little called Androskeag—Waukeag Neck. On July 15th, Little "lodged at Mr. Bean's—in good circumstances, generous and kind." Little crossed Flanders Bay by boat from Waukeag Neck to Gouldsboro, where he met with one of the original English inhabitants, a Colonel Jones, who resided "at the head of a cove on the East by land of Gouldeboro." The precise location is unclear, as Little, in his 1788 letter to Samuel Phillips, claimed to have traveled as far east as Narraquagus, which is quite a distance (twenty miles) from modern Gouldsboro town and bay. Colonel Jones was accommodating, allowing Little to write a quick letter home before Jones set sail for the south. At the same time, he was a man of great wealth—and very proud of it! "He is much taken up with this vain world," Little wrote, surrounded by the natural beauty of forested islands and hills and blue-green waters. "How many poor rich unhappy creatures there are who struggle in the feeble attempt to serve God and Mammon." Little "advised . . . moderation."[28]

The next day Little re-crossed the bay to visit another of the original grantees of the 12 lots, a Mr. Simpson, who lived

---

28 Varney, *Gazetteer*, 267, 311; *Journal*, 1774, 26; Little, "General Account of the Rise and Progress of the Eastern Mission."

at "saltwater falls," presumably where he had a saw or grist mill. There was a meeting house at this unnamed place on Waukeag Neck. "Mr. Simpson is [in] great affliction, almost lost the sight of both his eyes. It gives me joy to comfort the afflicted." On the Sabbath, a great crowd of people attended the meetinghouse. It was a "serious audience," though, unhappily, included people from throughout the region of Waukeag Neck and Sullivan who could not break through an unnamed disagreement to unite in a self-sustaining parish. After the meeting the pastor was again aboard a boat or canoe heading north up Taunton Bay to near the town of what today is Franklin. He stayed with Abram Donnell, one of the original settlers, whose family had experienced much sickness. He preached and baptized at Mr. Hardison's, another early settler, then departed south from Taunton Bay, returning to Waukeag Neck for more services, more baptisms. Amid this flurry of activity, the parson experienced uncertainty about God's will and his mission to fulfill the Great Commission: "the more I labour for the good of others, the more peace and comfort within. I hope I am not sent here in vain."[29]

Many people during the past two centuries have followed in the wake of Daniel Little's next stop on his missionary tour: Mount Desert Island. Little boarded a schooner that set out from Waukeag Neck for a voyage of about six miles. Aboard the vessel was James Richardson, one of the original English settlers of Mount Desert Island, and another man, whom Little refused to name because of his infamy: "half distracted, dreadfully profane. Oh how vile

---

29 Varney, *Gazetteer*, 238, 531-532; *Journal*, 1774, 27.

and hard," Little exclaimed, "does human nature appear, when learning and good sense is prostituted to the service of the Devil." Once upon the isle, Little "preached to a very numerous and serious assembly." In the afternoon, he journeyed by boat to the northwest to a thin stretch of the Mt. Desert Narrows, perhaps the island of Thompson, where he spoke to people "zealous to attend Prayer." The pastor was so busy coming and going, meeting and preaching, that he barely had a chance to observe the beauty of his surroundings: craggy coast, forested hills, quiet bays, inlets, and ponds. Subsequently, he took a boat toward Gouldsboro but the winds died, and the sails slackened. They were becalmed in Frenchman's Bay for hours, only arriving late at night at Waukeag Neck. Along the way, "fatigued by the labours of this week," Little slept. Once the morning of July 22nd broke, he took a boat to Gouldsboro, where he rested and took bearings of his work: "When I review my path I see great defects in wisdom and fortitude. But more unfeigned love to Christ, and the honour & success of his gospel which I am allowed to preach, is my heart's desire."[30]

With renewed energy, Daniel Little set off by horseback the next morning, July 23rd, on his way to the northwest to what he called the Western Bay, probably Flanders Bay. This was "the first time mounting a horse and finding a horse road in all this country," he wrote happily, grateful for the chance of the exercise. He arrived and stayed with a Baptist named Mr. Charles, who became Little's guide crossing the neck of land between Flanders Bay and Long Cove. Here, Little lodged with a Capt. Nichols. People from the eastern

---

30 Varney, *Gazetteer*, 378; *Journal*, 1774, 27-28.

Flanders Bay and western Long Cove arrived at the Captain's house for religious services. The pastor asked the Baptist to read a Psalm, but he did so in such an ignorant, blundering fashion that Little could not contain his outrage, at least in his journal: "How much grace he might have in his heart, I know not, but the lowest for genius, learning or manners that ever I knew who assumed the character of a public Preacher." A Baptist, he railed about the importance of baptism, but Little could find little depth in his thinking. "Such men are to be pitied and prayed for, who take the flights of a wild and disordered brain for the genuine dictates of wisdom and the much to be desired noble elevation of the Holy Spirit of God." Fortunately, the errant teacher was on his way traveling to some other place: "so that I hope," wrote Little, "the innocent and ignorant will escape the confusion that seemed likely to take place."[31]

For the next week, Little made no record in his journal; one imagines that he tried to regain his peace of mind amid the breeze blowing off the bay cooling the warmth of the July pine and birch forest. Partially refreshed, perhaps, he departed south, by horseback still, though on the first day of August he became "very tired and faint in the thick woods, not a breath of air, not a dry thread in my shirt. Rested and cool'd myself in the afternoon; in the evening a little refreshed." His goal in this laborious activity was to visit "places to which my labours in a former appointment," two years before in 1772, "did not extend." Returning to Colonel Jones east of Flanders Bay, he met with a man and woman whom he had seen two years before; they wished to renounce

---

31 *Journal*, 1774, 28-29.

their errors and embrace Christ, which they did. Such rewards continued to inspire Little, whose object became the peninsula between Union and Jordan river, formerly called lot Number One, in time the town of Trenton. He intended to voyage to this region on August 3rd, but then a person arrived at Colonel Jones's from Mount Desert, begging the pastor to return, as the people wanted to hear more. Little relented and traveled to the island. "Many of the hearers appeared deeply touched by the word, and begged another sermon in the morning" of the 4th, to which Little agreed. The next morning, the people "showed a great desire of the stated means of grace," and wanted to publicly thank the pastor for his work. Little nipped this in the bud, telling them that "if they had received any benefit by my instruction, to give the glory to God, and said I would mention their grateful sense of the care of the Province to the Trustees" who had sent him. The enthusiasm of the hearers was due in part to the religious conflict on the island between "Baptists & others"; there was one man, called "Minister Young," who was a lay preacher who tended to unite the people. Minister Young led an "exemplary life and religious improvement of the Sabbath"; he "was universally beloved, generous, catholic and open in his sentiments, kind, pious and popular in his behaviour." His character was such that Little believed that "if I could have tarried a while over the Sabbath there was a fair prospect of gathering them into one Church." Instead, Minister Young and another man conveyed Little by canoe a half mile across the Narrows to his original goal, the Jordan River.[32]

---

32 *Journal*, 1774, 30

The Jordan is a small tidal river that flows into the Mount Desert Narrows. Little stayed with a Mr. Wescott, where he preached to the family and neighbors. Wescott had twelve children, only half of whom had been baptized. Wescott had "denied" younger children "the privilege from a doubt of the appointment being from heaven," which Little thought a singular idea. He convinced Wescott of his error, and the children were baptized in, as it were, the tears of repentance of the father. Wescott became a follower, joining Little by boat on a fifteen-mile journey southwest into the Narrows, then north into Union River Bay, proceeding into the mouth up the river "in order to keep Sabbath." Little stayed with Justice Jordan, as he had when first arriving in early July. Although Little felt "considerable fatigue," he felt compelled to grant these people, who longed for a permanent pastor, "another Sabbath." The industrious Union River folk were "raising a sawmill," perhaps as an antidote to the melancholy of the place, as death had been a frequent visitor. Alcoholism was quite a problem, the occasion for one of the deaths. After the worship service, and funeral, the people appeared quite humbled.[33]

At this point in his travels, Daniel Little decided it was time to journey further west, to Blue Hill, which he had visited in 1772, as well as "the Western harbor, of Mount Desert," the object being "to visit a few families greatly remote from all others." He attempted to depart by boat from Weymouth Point, at the mouth of the Union River, but contrary wind forced a delay. Little visited dying Mr. Weymouth again, and "took lodgings at Capt. Williams to

---

33 Ibid., 31-32.

be ready for the tide in the morning." On August 9th, Little set off in a rowboat with two rowers and a few passengers, one of whom was James Richardson, another a son of Mr. Wescott, for the western shores of Mount Desert Island. After about six hours of rowing, they arrived at a cove on the southern side of the island, "which almost cuts the Isle in two." They rowed up this broad inlet into Somes Sound, where Richardson lived.[34]

The Richardson family had arrived from Cape Ann at the end of the French Indian War, during which Richardson had served as a private in the militia. Richardson had reconnoitered Mount Desert Island, and had built a simple "pole house" in anticipation of relocating his family there. He brought his family, journeying by boat with two others, in December; it had taken him a fortnight to sail up the coast from Cape Ann to the Penobscot, whereupon he attempted to enter Somes Sound. It must have been a daunting prospect, arriving in dim December light among "hideous mountains," in Little's words. The boats confronted ice at the mouth of the sound, which "overset" Richardson's "vessel." Somehow, he and his family survived the wreck, salvaged supplies, and made their way with two other families to the Cranberry Islands, "which made one side of the harbour at the mouth of the river," or sound. Half a dozen small islands lie southeast of the sound. Richardson and his family and friends survived the winter on their meager supplies, which included cattle. With spring, and the thawing of the ice, Richardson journeyed by canoe thirty miles to get his family "one bushel of corn." They relocated to the head

---

34 Ibid., 32.

of the sound, where they began new lives. Richardson and wife Rachel had "6 small children" when they made this adventure. Over the next decade, Rachel bore five more children. They had some neighbors, such as the Somes family, which had arrived to the sound which bears their name about the same time as the Richardsons. Other families lived on the northeast part of the island, eight miles away, through "a trackless and mountainous wood."[35]

Arriving among these people ten years later in August, 1774, Rev. Daniel Little married Richardson's daughter, Rachel, named for her mother, to Wescott's son, David, on the afternoon of August 9th. Such families of Mount Desert Island, in and about the Penobscot Bay, and all along coastal Maine, survived the elements and periodic privation by a deep faith in God. They spent their lives in work and prayer. Often lacking a church and congregation, the Bible was their solace, their chief form of instruction and entertainment, their guide for the vicissitudes of existence. James and Rachel Richardson spent their evenings reading from and discussing the Bible with their adult and young children, all gathered around, every one of the adult's holding their own Holy book.[36]

The nuptial vows completed, the pastor "refused taking any fees, as being inconsistent with the benevolent intention of the mission." James and Rachel Richardson, Richardson's brother, and one of their children, on August 11th boarded a "fishing schooner," and brought Daniel Little on board to

---

35 Ibid., 32-33; "Mount Desert Island: Shaped by Nature": http://mdi.mainememory.net/page/205/display.html

36 *Journal*, 1774, 32-33.

take him to Blue Hill, on the eastern side of the main peninsula of Penobscot Bay. Little intended to celebrate communion with the parishioners of the congregational church at Blue Hill, and the Richardson's wanted to participate. They set off into headwinds and fog that restricted their movements to only six miles. They anchored at Southwest Harbor, went ashore and supped at J. C. Cockle's home. Cockle had come to the island the year before, in 1773, as part of an attempt by the proprietor of the island, Francis Bernard, Governor of Massachusetts, to settle Germans on his lands. After "refreshment," Little and his friends "returned to the boat and put up for the night. Slept comfortable all night," though the boat was cramped, "and better for not sleeping one wink the night before."[37]

They set off again in the morning, rowing the schooner furiously against the headwind; it took all morning to finally reach the open sea, where with sails set they beat against the wind round the southern points of Mount Desert Island. Eventually coming around Lopaus Point heading northwest, they achieved a following wind and made good time toward Blue Hill Bay, a picturesque place of forested shores and islands and a small hill rising above. Arriving at the bay, the wind died and they experienced "a profound calm." Little, anxious to feel land again, "went ashore at the first house I could find." It belonged to Samuel Foster, one of the first inhabitants of the southern part of Blue Hill, a promontory, Naskeag Point, that jutted into the Penobscot Bay between Deer Isle, Mount Desert Island, and Long Island. The next morning, back aboard the schooner, Little and his nautical

---

37 Ibid., 33-34; *Bangor Historical Magazine*, 5(1889): 1-3.

companions made it by noon to the town of Blue Hill. Little reunited with friends made two years before in 1772, chief of whom was Captain Joseph Woods, the first settler of this region at the end of the French-Indian War. Little inquired of his friend about "the state of the Church which I gathered when here last." He had sent a letter ahead of his visit to ready themselves for communion, courtesy in part of "Elder [Enoch] Titcomb of Newbury" who "by my desire last year had sent them a donation of proper communion vessels." Preparing for the Sabbath the next morning, Little retired early to his chamber at the home of Captain Woods. "Oh! Sweet retirement, meditation, and prayer must have their time; it is necessary for the refreshment and strength of the mind as rest in sleep for the body." Little blamed his extraordinary fatigue and impaired health on "so many removes in open boats & different lodgings, etc."[38]

Sabbath morning, August 14th, Rev. Little "preached to a full house, and administered the holy Supper for the edification & encouragement of the numerous young people & others." The sacrament "was a solemn, friendly, and to some, a joyful communion." The congregation had tried to locate a permanent pastor without success, which inspired Little to pledge to "tarry one Sabbath more with them, and preach a Lecture on Tuesday." He would engage in private visits, but otherwise needed rest. Indeed, the next day Little was "very poorly, with pain in my head, and faintness." Recovered on Tuesday the 16th, Little journeyed south by horse ("the only horse in town, and the only one in all the 6

---

38 *Journal*, 1774, 33-34; R. G. F. Candage, *Historical Sketch of Bluehill, Maine* (Ellsworth, ME: Hancoock County Publishing Co., 1905), 7, 9.

Western townships") to a forested area the locals called "Birch Land," where he lectured to different families of the region. He then proceeded a few miles "to the head of the Salt Pond," which adjoins Little Blue Hill Bay by means of a cataract called Fire Falls. He lodged with one of the local families, then returned the next day to Capt. Wood's. On the 18th, Little rode along the Little Blue Bay, and visited Colonel Nathan Parker, one of the original inhabitants of the town. He was a veteran of the French-Indian War, having been part of the militia contingent that attacked Louisburg at Cape Breton Island; he was brother-in-law to Joseph Woods.[39]

Little's travels and meetings and lectures, in which he visited numerous families, very serious and pious, who sought more religious edification, were a prelude to the celebration of the Sabbath, August 21st. Little felt that the community was coming together in "friendly converse" that "gives an openness to Religion, and is of advantage in removing the doubts, scruples, temptations, and sinful shame that many poor souls are subject to." Little preached before "a crowded assembly," which included visitors from Jordan's River, Mount Desert Island, and Naskeag Point. The service featured "full communion" and "8 children baptized." Little and the people of these parts had experienced a "personal friendship formed upon religious principles," which Little believed "looks toward Heaven for its completion and perpetuity." He had "looked into the state of the afflicted, to scatter their gloomy fears, and regulate

---

39 *Journal*, 1774, 34-35; Varney, *Gazetteer*, 121-122; Candage, *Historical Sketch of Bluehill*, 51.

their sorrow." In this work, his own tribulations, of loss of children and spouse, gave him a sense of empathy toward others, to feel their pain, to counter pain with joy.[40]

After the meeting, Little was off, traveling south, no doubt in Richardson's schooner, making harbor at Herrick's Bay near Naskeag Point. He spent the night, and held a service for the locals on Monday, August 22nd. One woman present, whom Little had met previously, had two young disabled children, whom she had allowed to bind her "down with many sorrows." This time, however, with Little's help, she kissed "the rod with joy"—and the boys were baptized. From here Little traveled south and west around Naskeag Point, arriving at the mouth of the Benjamin River, where the town of Sedgwick was located. Here Little preached and baptized, then crossed the narrow strait to Deer Isle, where he lodged with Captain William Eaton, and preached and baptized at a "house of affection." August 25th, Little went by boat along the coast of Deer Isle to Northwest Harbor, where he lodged with one of the many Haskell's of the island. August 27th, Little set off in a whaleboat rowed by four oarsmen across the East Penobscot Bay to the evergreen-studded Fox Islands, where he stayed with an elderly couple, Ezekiel Kent and his wife Susanna. In their house lived their oldest daughter, Penelope, "husbandless with three children, by a sudden death." About the same time that her husband, Josiah Winslow, died, Ezekiel and Susanna's oldest son Ezekiel, suddenly drowned—and he was the one "on whom they chiefly depended for support." The elder Ezekiel's brothers had died in the West Indies, and

---

40 *Journal*, 1774, 35.

Susanna's first husband and their only son was also deceased. It was, therefore, a "house of great affliction." Little wrote in his journal, "but few people seem to know where to depend fully for support in trouble, or how to rise with increasing strength in the Lord, as afflictions press." Perhaps the Kent family knew how, or at least perhaps they did after listening to the pastor's counsel. "God seems to take delight," he said, "to show his tender mercy to kindle & not quench the smoking flax, to strengthen and not break the bruised reed; to revive the spirit of the contrite." Little knew from experience of the mercy of the Lord during transient human suffering.[41]

The next morning was the Sabbath. Little preached at the home of Captain Joseph Waterman, a sea captain and resident of Vinalhaven. The number of people, their religiosity and sensibility, surprised Little. They "are in the midst of their wheat harvest," Little reported, and "have lost such grain by the wet & fogg [sic]." Their crop was enough to sustain themselves, with little remaining for trade. There were very few sawmills up and down the coast. In short, the people had to rely on fishing. That afternoon he crossed "in a small sail boat" back over the bay to Deer Isle—actually an archipelago of forested, rocky islands. Here he visited families, married a couple, and preached. A young minister whom Little had befriended, one Reed, took a birch bark canoe to Blue Hill to preach in Little's stead, while the pastor stayed at Northwest Harbor, lodging with a Mr. Webb, perhaps Seth Webb, a noted pioneer and hunter in the region.

---

41 *Journal*, 1774, 35-36; L. Vernon Briggs, *History of Shipbuilding on North River, Plymouth County, Massachusetts* (Boston: Coburn Brothers, 1889), 379.

The night of September 3rd was rainy; Little, along with fifteen others, lodged with Webb; the "house very leaky" and "the bed clothes wet." As a result Little "slept but very little."[42]

For a town without a pastor, or even an organized church, it is remarkable that Deer Isle had a meetinghouse—of what size or dimensions or location or origins are unanswerable questions. Perhaps the influence of missionary Oliver Noble, who came among these people the previous year (1773), was the inspiration. Daniel Little preached and "administered the holy Supper" on September 4th. He baptized an amazing "23 children and two adults," and formed a church of twenty-seven people. "The Meeting house today crowded—Ab[ou]t 60 females in the isle, and many strangers" from surrounding islands. "The Church behaved very solemn—spectators of the congregation very orderly." The service lasted until the afternoon, in part because "strangers took up so much time for conversation in the intermission." All was good. "I hope this day will be the beginning of many happy days on this Isle. It gives me satisfaction that the two churches here—Blue Hill and, now, Deer Isle—that stand at distance of near a hundred miles from the nearest Western Churches" of the lower Maine coast "have had a first and happy time for shewing forth their Lord's death according to his appointment."[43]

September 5th, Little journeyed to the northeast part of

---

42 *Journal*, 1774, 36-37; Charles E. Waterman, *The Maine Watermans* (Mechanic Falls, ME: Ledger Publishing Co., 1906), 55; George L. Hosmer, *An Historical Sketch of the Town of Deer Isle, Maine* (Boston: Stanley and Usher, 1886), 122.

43 *Journal*, 1774, 37-38; *Bangor Historical Magazine*, 1(1886), 140.

the isle to Captain Eaton's, where he provided another worship service that included baptizing four children. From hence, he journeyed with Captain Eaton in a birchbark canoe northwest past Little Deer Isle, around Cape Rosier, on to the mouth of the Bagaduce River, where he stayed with a Captain Butemans at Goose Falls. It was a moist, wooded region of cool nights and warm days in September. Here, Little again "preached, and baptized 13 children." He married a young couple, Ephraim Blake and Mary Colson, then crossed the mouth of the Bagaduce (Little called the river, Major Bagaduce) to Castine, which Little referred to as Perkins, named for the original English inhabitant, Captain John Perkins, who had come to this region from York about six years before. From Perkins (or Castine), Little went with two canoe-men up the river after nightfall. "The current made strong against us, besides 4 rapids of narrows to pass by, towing the boat, which made it late before we reached the inhabitants." Little was anticipating being the first Protestant missionary to these people at the head of the Bagaduce River; he did not want to disappoint, so he pushed himself by night. He ended up at the head of the western branch of the river, probably what is today called Mills Point. Here he preached and "baptized 6 children." Rev. Reed, who crossed by land from Blue Hill, joined the pastor. Little stayed at Samuel Gray's home. At this small settlement on the Bagaduce River, there were "15 families and 75 souls."[44]

Daniel Little departed, returning down the Bagaduce to

---

44 *Journal*, 1774, 38-39; George A. Wheeler, *History of Castine, Penobscot, and Brooksville, Maine* (Bangor, ME: Burr & Robinson, 1875), 206-207.

Perkins, where he stayed with a Mr. Grindle, who, he told the pastor, had once survived on "clams and potatoes" before their crops were harvested. From Grindle's he journeyed to the home of Captain Joseph Perkins, another of the original English inhabitants of Castine, with whom Little had stayed in 1772. "Spent the day in meditation & writing," thinking, "how pleasant [is] retirement. I wish I had prized it more when it was every day at my option," wrote the man who spent so much of his time on the move. "My body much fatigued for want of rest such more than my mind. To instruct, reprove and make happy my fellow creatures is my dayly [sic] joy." Recovering while serving the Lord, Little stayed at Joseph Perkins's for several days, during which he celebrated the Sabbath, on a "fine, pleasant morning." A large congregation of people joined together in worship in a barn of a local resident; Little "baptized 7 children." He felt somewhat recovered, this day of September 11th, but noted that some of the congregation did not look well. He blamed it on "the severe labour, with the love of Bacchus," which made these "earthy sensual creatures" suffer more than otherwise. Little thought it a shame, that humans, given the authority by God to exercise control over the Creation, should neglect their bodies as well as the "fertile soil" and "so respectable a river" as the Bagaduce. Humans must be better than the Creation, if they are to lord over it. What good is a slothful master? But, Little considered of these people, "upon the whole I think they are reforming." This good man, who practiced what he preached, visited the next day a "family whose poverty prevented their bringing their children to public meeting. Baptized 5 of them."[45]

Tuesday, September 13th, as he was wont to do, Daniel Little lectured to the people, providing "every weighty argument for the encouragement of the gospel ministry among them." This region of Castine and the Bagaduce River was fertile, some of the people wealthy, the land hosting about one hundred families. There were "7 coasting sloops owned in the river, a good navigation 9 miles from the mouth" of the river into Penobscot Bay. "The soil as good as any of the 12 townships" east and west of Union River. The people of the Bagaduce "are first in settlement," in terms of numbers—"and yet the people inert, timorous and divided about the place and importance of public worship." Perhaps this explained how they could not take full responsibility over this beautiful part of Creation. Little hoped that the arrival of new settlers with fresh energy along with his message about the importance of yielding from the Creation—natural as well as human—its full potential would "give a new and goodly face to this people." Nevertheless, Little felt a bit frustrated, considering that this was his second visit to the place—compared to Blue Hill these people of the Bagaduce were lagging behind. A church established at Blue Hill, and now at Deer Isle—there should be one established here, but not yet: too much envy among the people, and envy is a destroyer of religious sentiment.[46]

At this point in his journey, Little intended to ascend the Penobscot River, and planned, on September 14[th], to travel north to Fort Pownall, but for the wind. Instead he visited

---

45 *Journal*, 1774, 39.

46 Ibid., 39-40.

more families, including "one good old saint ab[ou]t . . . 70, without husband or children, dependent on the charity of neighbours, whose Christian behaviour commanded the respect, honor and generosity of all that were sensible of her worth." The wind relented the next day; Little joined Captain John Perkins on the brief voyage from Castine north to Fort Pownall. The fort, built on a dramatic point jutting into the river, known originally as Wasaumkeag, was about fifteen years old, built during the French-Indian War by Governor Pownall as a means of securing the Penobscot River and intimidating the French and their Indian allies. Today a state park commemorates Fort Pownall. Visitors can see the remains of the foundation of the blockhouse that once housed British-American soldiers. A lighthouse, built in 1836, adds to the picturesque beauty of Penobscot Bay and Penobscot River. Here, Little joined Jedidiah Preble's son Captain John Preble, who knew the waters of the Penobscot, and the people, better than any of the English, having served as a guide for exploring expeditions, such as that of James Chadwick ten years before in 1764. Preble led the pastor upstream by birchbark canoe, through the Penobscot Narrows to Colonel Jonathan Buck's, what became the town of Bucksport, Maine; Buck was a pioneer settler from Haverhill, Massachusetts. From Buck's, the men paddled twenty miles upriver, staying with a Captain Cobb at a place called by Little, "Sawardobscot," his transliteration for Sowadabscook, a river that flows into the Penobscot at modern Hampden. Little was "cold and tired," and could do little but sleep. The next morning, the journey continued to Captain John Brewer's, what became the town of Brewer, Maine. Captain Brewer's home was about five miles below the falls and the head of tide of the Penobscot. Little stayed at Brewer's for several days, becoming acquainted with an itinerant preacher who had been there a few months, Isaac Knowles—"a sensible, well disposed young man" who had attended Harvard. Knowles divided his time between the people of Brewer, and the people of Marsh Bay, or Frankfort, a dozen miles downriver. Little celebrated the Sabbath at the confluence of the Penobscot with the Kenduskeag River, at the home of a Captain Smart. "The people on this river," he wrote, "are very dissimilar in their education and outward circumstances. Some of good life, sense and known virtue, some quite the reverse." Little noted in his journal that "one Canadian Indian came to public worship." The following morning, Little went by canoe with Captain Smart as his guide upriver to the falls, modern Bangor, which was the farthest north that English settlement extended; here, Captain Preble lived. Little hoped to visit the Penobscot Indians, whom he was informed would be found at "the French master for the Indian trade at the head of the tide or falls." The people being absent, he began the return journey with Captain Smart to Kenduskeag, but about three miles along, the wind and rain forced them to return to their original destination at Captain Preble's. Preble informed the pastor that from their location at the head of tide to Fort Pownall is thirty-three miles, and from the fort to Owl's Head is thirty miles. Owl's Head is a promontory that juts into Penobscot Bay opposite the Fox Islands. Little described its location as "on the mainland of Waldo's patent between St. Georges & said [Penobscot] Bay."[47]

That afternoon of September 19th, Captain Jonathan Lowder, stationed at Fort Pownall and well-known and liked by the indigenous people, guided Rev. Little down the west side of the Penobscot River, on foot, two miles, when they spied several dozen Penobscot across the river. They called them for a means of conveyance, and a young man, named Persock, paddled over in a birchbark canoe and brought the captain and parson across the river. The people whom Little came among were a disturbing lot: "found ab[ou]t 20 young and old, and near half of them so drunk as to be incapable of seeing, hearing, speaking or moving—dead drunk. The others (besides said Persock) speaking, laughing or frowning or strutting or jumping. About 7 of them Canadians, the others the dregs or remains of the old Penobscot tribe. I soon left them, as being incapable of any instruction." Little and Lowder journeyed down the eastern side of the river, "visited several new settlements," and crossed back over and ascended to Preble's, who was in charge of the "truck house," that is, the supplies of food and clothing that the English exchanged to the Indians for furs."[48]

That evening, Persock arrived at Preble's to speak with Rev. Little. The pastor described him as "a young Canadian 19 years . . . , dress'd partly in French habit." He spoke French, but Little made use of a bilingual Frenchman who worked at the truck house. Through the interpreter, Persock

---

47 Ibid., 40-41; Varney, *Gazetteer*, 9556-557; James McLachlan, *Princetonians, 1748-1768: A Biographical Dictionary* (Princeton, NH: Princeton University Press, 2015), 647. Waldo's Patent was originally a huge proprietary land grant between the Muscongus and Penobscot rivers.

48 *Journal*, 1774, 41-42.

told Little that he and his parents had arrived from Quebec six weeks earlier, that "his grandmother in all probability, was a Bradley by name, and when young taken from Penacook," along the Merrimack River, "in a former War. The mother has English features; and is doubtful of her being of Indian origin altogether. Tho' she was delivered of child the other night, abroad in the rain," she was "well the next day in the Truck house," where trade occurred. Little pronounced this ability to recover quickly from parturition, "Indian by art, if not by nature." Persock had been baptized a Catholic when six years old; he had been educated in part by the French. Little questioned him about his religious beliefs. Persock believed in the sacrament of confession, that his sins—"bad words, actions, and tho'ts," though "he had so many," were forgiven. He had not received confession for three months, since departing from Quebec. Little wondered whether Persock was worried about those, unconfessed sins. "When sick or great way off and can't go to the Priest, I believe in no danger, I am not afraid of my sin." But why? "For I pray to God, (said he) every night and evening" for "God to pardon all my sins, and when I die to receive me to paradise." Little thought Persock had the makings of a Protestant, and wished for him to join the pastor so that he could be so educated; perhaps he could become a missionary to his own people. But Persock said that he doubted his parents would let him. Little asked Persock to bring his parents to him, which he did the next morning. Indeed, the parents would in no way allow their son to leave them, and Persock said, "can't go against Parents." Little asked, "will you come and live with me when you are free?" Persock responded, "never free with us Indians, never free from

Parents till we are married." "I pity the poor fellow," Little confided to his journal, "he appears to have more innocency and integrity than all the rest, and his conscience will not let him disobey his Parents," though it "might deliver him from those temptations and superstitions that may finally ruin him," because, Little cried out to his journal, the Penobscot have sunk into "filth, folly, & beastly nastiness and intemperance." Little had no doubt that superficial Catholicism contributed to these failings. He prayed that the English, being Protestants, would show justice and temperance toward these people.[49]

The autumnal equinox, Little set forth from Preble's trading station, and the "dreadful ugly, yet to be pitied Penobscot tribe," for Fort Pownall. The tide and wind cooperated, along with a good canoe with four paddlers, so that they reached the fort that evening around dusk. Colonel Thomas Goldthwaite, the commander of the fort, offered quarters for Little, who spent the next day with the colonel. The following morning Little was off again, up the Orland River, which flows into the Penobscot, then northwest up the Eastern Channel of the Penobscot to Captain Buck's. September 23rd, Little, with the help of a guide, a Major Moore, visited the families along the Eastern Channel. He discovered that many of the people of the area were filled with rancor toward others. Little engaged in "private converse" with many people, hoping to remove "some painful suspicions and jealousies in point of honor or interest among neighbours." September 25th, the Sabbath, Little, after a day of rest, was ready to lead the people of the Eastern

---

[49] Ibid., 42-43.

Channel and the region around Bucksport and Franklin in worship. Captain Buck's house provided the venue, to which "a large and very serious congregation" of people gathered. Little "baptized 8 children," then preached again, "by the desire of the neighbours," that evening. Little discovered that his work the previous Friday had removed the "rash and angry vows," so that the people "united decently in the worship of God." It felt good to be a peacemaker.[50]

Monday, Little journeyed back down the Eastern Channel toward the fort, staying with the physician and chaplain of Fort Pownall, Dr. William Crawford. Little "visited by the Dr.'s desire, several of his patients, truly pitiable and distressing cases in surgery; two with their thigh bones laid open 3 or 4 inches, and one under care near a year. The Dr. appears a bold and dexterous Surgeon." He was as well quite a naturalist, and knew the correct potions to give the sick. Generally, he reported to Little, the climate of the Penobscot was such that there were few illnesses. Crawford was well read, and showed excellent judgment, such that he impressed Little sufficiently to recommend that he leave the fort for some more useful occupation, such as working "as a Surgeon among the numerous dependent poor," there being no such person along the entire Maine coast from Muscongus Bay to Machias Bay. Tuesday morning, Little preached at the chapel of the fort, and "baptized 15 children." That same morning, a delegation arrived from the town of Belfast, southwest of Fort Pownall at the mouth of the Passagassawakeag River. They took the parson to their town in a canoe paddled by four men. Belfast was founded

---

50 Ibid., 43-44.

by ethnic Irish from Londonderry, New Hampshire. They purchased part of the Waldo patent, and had made a thriving town. The population had doubled since Little had been with the people two years before. They devoted their attention to husbandry rather than the lumber business, which Little thought was most advisable—hence they grew more than enough food, and avoided the consequence of too heavy a reliance on lumber mills: "intemperance, especially in Rum drinking." The parson preached for the people of Belfast on a Thursday; everyone from the town (save one) attended. Little "baptized 6 children."[51]

Friday morning, September 30th, Daniel Little set forth from Belfast to the south by canoe with four men paddling toward what he called "Long Island, or Winslow's Island," now known as Isleboro. When they departed, the bay was calm, but soon, as rain cleared, the wind came up from the west off of the mountains around Camden, creating some swells that were difficult to negotiate. They put in at a small island, perhaps Seal Island, till the wind calmed, then set forth for the southern portion of this long chain of islands in the western part of Penobscot Bay. Eventually they reached Isleboro, putting in, perhaps, at Crow Cove, then walking along the beach to the town center, situated in the northern part of the southernmost part of Long Island. Little stayed with one of the first settlers, Jonathan Parker, whom Little described as "the agent for Mr. Winslow the proprietor of the island." Isaac Winslow owned the island, but lived in Massachusetts. Parker was "a sensible Gent. from Connecticut of good family & fortune who by losses at sea

---

51 Ibid., 44-46.

was reduced to nothing." He arrived at the island in 1771, and "now cuts 10 tons of English hay ab[ou]t his own door. The Island is a garden of soil." Little had, it appears, visited the island previously, in 1772, having corresponded with Winslow about "the best method of settling the Island for the better interest of the people, his profit, and especially for the advancement of Religion." Winslow, apparently, used the island merely for profit, leasing the land to settlers without concern for religion. Parker informed Little as much, and told the pastor that the settlers were a discontented lot, wanting to make their town a good Christian place for families. But they needed the proprietor to take an interest in helping to settle a pastor among them. So far, Winslow had refused to do so. "What an earthly and heavenly Paradise would this Island be," Little wrote, "if the settlers were proprietors, holy and righteous, and furnished with a godly Minister & Magistrate; walking in the faith and fellowship of the gospel."[52]

The first day of October, Little stayed with Nathaniel Palmer, another early settler. "After so many changes and converse with different educations and manners," Little wrote, retrospectively, "it is pleasant to sit down with a middle-aged pious Family, whose faith, patience and love shine thro' their trials and hardships—and great the pleasure and profit such souls of hidden worth have in relating the various dealings of the Lord in providence." The Palmer family expressed to Little their sense of "God's goodness, his fatherly kindness," which they experienced through "the

---

52 Ibid., 46; John P. Farrow, *History of Islesborough, Maine* (Bangor, ME: Burr, 1893), 14, 28, 93.

rod of reproof which his own children need." Little, too, had felt the rod of love: "My numerous and singular trials have given me a useful feeling for my dear brethren in every place." October 2nd, "the first Sabbath of public worship" ever experienced "on the Island" occurred at Palmer's house. Little performed the sacraments of baptism and marriage. He learned from Palmer that the proprietor Winslow had offered a prospective pastor one hundred acres of land to settle among the people. There having been no takers, Palmer hoped that Little would in time meet with Winslow to let him know that the terms of employing such a minister must change; there had to be a more lucrative offer. "Nothing should I do with more cheerfulness," Little wrote in his journal, "if I live to wait upon that Gent. [Winslow] whom the settlers esteem, and ascribe his mistake to his dependence upon interested men for advice."[53]

Little set forth in a schooner from Long Island on October 3rd intent on crossing West Penobscot Bay to Camden. Once they arrived at Camden Harbor, the wind swooped down from the inland hills, bringing a squall, which forced the captain of the schooner to run before the wind to a little cove, where they anchored. Little went ashore, and walked to Major William Minot's home situated at the falls of Megunticook River. Minot, from Boston, ran a sawmill with his brother, who had died the previous years, sending his father into a "delirium." Such, wrote Little, are the "necessary . . . clouds of earthly glory in every part of the world," which bring people to the recognition of what is

---

53 *Journal*, 1774, 46-47; Farrow, *Islesborough*, 111.

really true.[54]

The next day, October 4th, Little hiked five miles (along what is today Route 1) to a small settlement at the mouth of a river, the harbor and bay being too rough for sailing or canoeing—hence the Indian name for the river, Megunticook, "great swells of the sea." Next to Clam Cove (called Glen Cove today, in Rockport, Maine), lived William Gregory, an early settler of the place, who kept "a public house of entertainment," where Little stayed for two days. Gregory and his neighbors, amounting to twenty families, had lived in this area, today's Rockport, for four years; they had "never heard a sermon before since their first settlement." To oblige them, Little preached and baptized. This last place on Little's 1774 missionary itinerary, he described as "30 miles from St. Georges [River] Westerly by water, & 7 by land," lying about "the middle of Penobscot bay on the West side." Little hoped "to proceed by land home if it was practicable without too much danger or fatigue." Gregory's tavern was the furthest south of any place on the peninsular necks of land between Penobscot Bay and the Kennebec River that a person could access by horse or on foot, following trail markers, a path that would take them by land down the coast; otherwise, travelers must go by boat up and down the coast, put in at bays or islands, then proceed by foot "to Pownalborough Court," on the Kennebec River, the northernmost courthouse along the

---

54 *Journal*, 1774, 47-48; John L. Locke, *Sketches of the History of the Town of Camden, Maine* (Hallowell, ME: Master, Smith & Co. 1859), 29.

Maine coast, "or [to] other business."[55]

Departing the Penobscot region October 5th, Little looked back on his three-month missionary excursion, calculating that he had traveled "by water chiefly in canoes 500 miles as my visits and labours have been up and down rivers & bays and athwart to uplands & islands." He had performed 253 baptisms. "The kind care of Providence" affected Daniel Little, who felt blessed that he had, throughout his journey, had "preservation of health and security from danger." During his last night at Gregory's Tavern, he had learned from people passing through, who lived at Frenchman's Bay (where Little had traveled in mid-July), that a "young man" who had then taken the pastor across the bay in a "cedar boat" had recently overset "in a squall in sight of his own door" and perished. Little, whose family experiences had made him familiar with the whims of Death, wondered: "Why has my life been preserved, but to redeem time and do more for God and religion."[56]

Little set forth by horseback toward the St. Georges River, staying along the way at an unnamed town, probably Thomaston. Here he discovered that the people were supplied with a minister for the Sabbath, and that, since he was in a hurry to return home, he would make a (for him, unusual) exception, and travel on the Sabbath. Saturday evening, there was a controversy in the town respecting the Boston Port Bill, and whether or not trade with Boston

---

55 *Journal*, 1774, 48; Locke, *Camden*, 63; Rose B. Waterman, *Maynard S. Bird: The Sage of a Maine Son* (Lincoln, NE: IUniverse, 2005), 3.

56 *Journal*, 1774, 48-49; Bourne, *History of Wells and Kennebunk*, 710.

should be carried on.[57] Little did his best to try to calm the arguers with words of "moderation and good order," which eventually prevailed. On the Sabbath, October 6th, he departed for Waldoboro on a horse he purchased that morning, perhaps from his "pilot," a Mr. Robbins. Little and his guide swam their horses across the St. Georges, then took the road to Waldoboro, perhaps following in the general path of today's Route 1. Little arrived, visited with Dr. Martin Shepherd, the "Dutch minister" of the town, then proceeded across the Medomak River by ferry, arriving at "a good English tavern" kept by a Mr. Ninals in a community with many German immigrants.[58]

The following morning, Little hired a guide to take him to the Damariscotta River. He traveled ten miles and crossed the river "at the head of the tide," then proceeded to the Sheepscot River, crossed it by means of a ferry, then continued on to Wiscasset, where he stayed with the local minister, a Mr. Moore, "a pleasant, sensible man." Rev. Moore presided over "an elegant Meeting house" in a town that was beautifully laid out, providing "a striking prospect from the town across the river." Little noted ships from Liverpool in the harbor. Wiscasset was in "the Easterly corner of the township of Pownalborough, ab[ou]t 12 miles from the Courthouse" on the Kennebec River. From Wiscasset, Little traveled to the Kennebec, crossing the ferry at Woolwich to the town of Bath. From Bath, Little

---

57 The Boston Port Bill, sometimes called the Coercive Acts or Intolerable Acts, was an action by the British government in response to the Boston Tea Party: it closed Boston harbor, suspended legislative government, and imposed martial law.

58 *Journal*, 1774, 49-50.

journeyed to Brunswick, staying at the tavern owned by Aaron Hinckley. Brunswick had experienced years of religious conflict owing to the large area of the town and the presence of two meetinghouses, on the west and east sides, which divided the congregation. Also, the people wavered between Congregationalism and Presbyterianism. Their minister, John Miller, invited Little to preach on the Sabbath, October 9th. Miller's "dwelling house 8 miles from this meeting house—greatly inconvenient." The congregation, Little noted, was "large and wealthy, but unhappily divided in sentiment, and about modes and forms of men's device." Little departed Rev. Miller's and journeyed to Stones Tavern on the Androscoggin River. Hurrying along, he stayed in Falmouth on October 10th and "set off early" on October 11th, reaching "home ab[ou]t 3 in afternoon." Daniel Little had been absent from home and parish "three months and eleven days."[59]

---

[59] Ibid., 50-51; George A. Wheeler, *History of Brunswick, Topsham, and Harpswell, Maine* (Brunswick, ME: Mudge, 1878), 773-774

4 THE PIOUS SCIENTIST

Upon Daniel Little's return to Kennebunk and the Second Parish of Wells, he found that his family were well, save for his daughter Margaret, "whose fits still continue," and his parishioners were likewise in health; only one person had died during his absence. "To find them and my house & interest under the care and preservation of divine Providence to this day calls aloud for devout thanks." Little's parishioners were an agricultural people, with few material interests, their property in goods rather than coin. The thriving nature of his parish was slightly threatened by happenings to the south. While Little was engaged in the lofty goals of the Great Commission on the eastern frontier, the people of Boston were engaged in a daily struggle for control of their thoughts and movements.

In the wake of the Treaty of Paris, the British Empire had quadrupled in size, requiring from the Parliament and King judicious and flexible responses to the challenge of a large empire comprised of English Protestants, French Catholics, and American Indian tribes. The English, attempting to maintain peace amid diversity and hard feelings, bringing disparate groups together to live as one, decided to impose upon their subjects various acts intended to bring order; the acts brought, instead, the American Revolution.

The British Stamp Act of 1765, the Tea Act of 1773, and the Coercive Acts of 1774 resulted in angry and violent responses from the thirteen colonies—and from the people of Maine. The Stamp Act, imposed by Parliament in 1765, was intended to defray the costs of the French-Indian War as well as help to pay for the administration of the British Empire in North America. It was a simple tax of a few pence upon legal documents and publications such as wills and newspapers. The British reasoned that the Americans could afford a few pence tax; besides, Americans were virtually tax-free, having never paid such taxes to the British. Patriots up and down the coast responded to the Stamp Act with the refrain, "no taxation without representation." Mobs burned tax men in effigy and tarred and feathered others. In Falmouth, opposition leaders seized stamps to hinder tax officials from doing their notorious job. Several years later the Tea Act placed a small tax on tea and gave the British East India Company a monopoly to market the tea to Americans. In Boston, the Sons of Liberty responded by descending upon a tea ship at Boston harbor and dumping the stuff into the sea. Mainers at York in imitation burned a tea cargo at York harbor. Falmouth residents openly proclaimed their refusal to drink British tea. The British responded to the tea parties with the Coercive Acts, called the Intolerable Acts in the colonies. The Coercive Acts punished Boston by closing Boston harbor to trade, suspending lawful government, and imposing martial law. Maine, as a part of Massachusetts, felt the pain of the Coercive Acts in two ways. Like other New England colonies, the Maine economy suffered a blow with the closing of Boston harbor. But more, Maine felt a close affinity to their fellow citizens of Massachusetts.

The sufferings of the people of Massachusetts in general and Boston in particular invited sympathy and charity. The people of the Second Parish of Wells, hitherto known for their charity, acted on behalf of those in need, while at the same time indicating how they leaned in politics, by raising a collection for the poor of Boston; this was December, 1774. Parish leaders believed that coin would be less precious than wood for heating and cooking, so sent 26 cords of wood, with the message that the "open and friendly commerce" of Boston, "we, on this eastern shore, more absolutely [depend] for support, than any other part of the Province. For your sake, and for our own, we prayerfully wait the kind interposition of Divine Providence, and the smiles of our gracious king for the redress of our general grievances; and in particular for the removal of the present obstruction to our trade with the town of Boston."[60]

During the spring of 1775, Divine Providence appeared oriented toward war rather than peace. In April of that year, British troops marched west from Boston toward Concord, facing colonial minutemen at Lexington and Concord. This bloody affair presaged further conflict, which was realized in June, when British troops sought to remove colonial militia from their bulwarks on the peninsula of Charlestown, south of Boston. The iron fist of war closed upon the colonies with the Battle of Bunker Hill. Little, his colleagues, and the parishioners of Maine responded, four days later, on June 21st, with a day of prayer, during which Daniel Little preached a sermon from the Old Testament book of Lamentations 3, 6: "He hath set me in dark places, as they that be dead of old." The veil of darkness descended upon the thirteen colonies, not to be lifted for eight years.[61]

---

60 *Journal*, 1774, 51; Bourne, *History of Wells and Kennebunk*, 468-469; *Records of the First Parish Church*.

61 Bourne, *History of Wells and Kennebunk*, 719.

At about the same time, the people of Machias, a small town on the northeastern coast on the Machias River, engaged in the first naval battle of the war. Two sloops and a ship "tender" under the command of Captain Ichabod Jones of Boston entered the Machias river in mid-June, 1775. They came to purchase timber for use of the British Army in Boston. In a threatening fashion, Captain Jones requested that he be allowed to load the wood aboard a British freighter. The townspeople of Machias, feeling like "prisoners of war," decided to resist. At first, they attempted to capture Captain Jones as he attended church on the Sabbath, but he escaped, as did the commander of the British warship *Margaretta*, which was anchored in the bay. Machias patriots were in pursuit, capturing the sloops, though the tender was able to escape to the mouth of the river. The next morning an engagement occurred between Machias patriots in a captured sloop and the soldiers of the tender. The captain of the latter was killed, and the weapons confiscated. The *Margaretta* was captured, the first such war prize of the American Revolution. The leader of the Maine patriots, Captain Jeremiah O'Brien, following up on the success at Machias, cruised the Bay of Fundy in a privateer, capturing two British schooners.

Nearer to home, from Daniel Little's perspective, was the British bombardment of Falmouth in the autumn of 1775. Casco Bay is a large harbor with many islands. For centuries travelers have stood at various locales surrounding the harbor, such as Cape Elizabeth, to view the dramatic and beautiful coast of rocky granite, spray rising from the unremitting waves crashing against the headland, fogs enveloping the water in the early morning, cormorants diving for fish, and the distant blue Atlantic. In time many lighthouses have dotted the bay warning arriving ships seeking the sanctuary of the bay. The Cape Elizabeth Lighthouse overlooks the southern part of Casco Bay, built on a rocky headland with a beautiful and slightly terrifying pounding surf. Henry Wadsworth Longfellow once stood at this cape and penned lines in witness of its dramatic beauty.

The sublimity of Casco Bay was interrupted one autumn day in 1775. The conflict between England and its colonies having begun a few months earlier, the British brought their strength to bear against the rebellious Americans. England, the greatest military and sea power in the world, boasting the largest navy in the world, could cruise American waters unmolested. Coastal inhabitants were terrified by the prospect of British marines invading their towns, burning, raping, and killing. The unthinkable appeared on the horizon to the inhabitants of Falmouth the morning of October 18. The British frigates *Canceau* and *Halifax* as well as two sloops and a "bomb ship" sailed into Casco Bay under the command of Captain Henry Mowat, who proclaimed to the inhabitants:

After so many premeditated attacks on the legal prerogatives of the best of Sovereigns, after the repeated instances you have experienced in Britain's long forbearance of the rod of correction, and the merciful and paternal extension of her hands to embrace you, again and again, have been regarded as vain and nugatory; and in place of a dutiful and grateful return to your King and parent state, you have been guilty of the most unpardonable rebellion, supported by the ambition of a set of designing men, whose insidious deeds have cruelly imposed on the credulity of their fellow-creatures, and at last have brought the whole into the same dilemma, which leads me to feel not a little the woes of the innocent of them, in particular on the present occasion, from my having it in orders to execute a just punishment on the Town of Falmouth. In the name of which authority, I previously warned you to remove without delay the human species out of the said Town, for which purpose I give you the time of two hours; at the period of which, a red pendant will be hoisted at the main topgallant mast head, with a gun. But should your imprudence lead you to show the least resistance, you will in that case free me of that humanity so strongly pointed out in my orders, as well as in my inclination. I also observe that all those who did, on a former occasion, fly to the King's ship under my command for protection, that the same door is now open and ready to receive them.[62]

Captain Mowat was already known to the inhabitants of Falmouth; they had several months before, when the *Canceau* appeared in the harbor, imprisoned him when he came on shore, though he was later released. Captain Mowat, seeking revenge with the approval of Admiral Greaves, opened fire the morning of the 18th, "all the vessels in the harbor" discharging "balls from three to nine pounds weight, bombs, carcasses, shells, grape shot, and musket balls." The attack lasted all day. Parties from the ships arrived on shore to set fire to buildings that escaped the bombardment. In all, 278 public and commercial buildings were destroyed and 136 private residences. The destruction of the town caused great suffering to its inhabitants, many of whom lost not only their home but all of their possessions, there having been little time between Mowat's arrival and the bombardment to remove them. Some townsmen turned to privateering during

---

62 Force, *American Archives*, 4th Series, III, 154.

the war to recover their losses and avenge the destruction of the town. These privateers had some success, but not as much as was desired and expected.

As dramatic an event of 1775 was Colonel Benedict Arnold leading a thousand militia up the Kennebec and Dead rivers and then through Canada for an assault on Quebec. Canada, made a British province at the close of the French-Indian War, did not join the thirteen colonies in their rebellion against England. Particularly the Canadian settlements along the St. Lawrence River were of prime importance to the American war effort. From Canada the British could launch repeated assaults on all of New England and New York. Hence the capture of Quebec and Montreal at the beginning of the war seemed essential to American war strategists. General George Washington, Commander in Chief of the American forces, adopted the strategy of quickly bringing the war to Canada with a two-pronged assault. He ordered General Richard Montgomery to journey up Lake Champlain to make an assault on Montreal. At the same time Colonel Benedict Arnold was to march along an eastern line to Quebec. Arnold was a young merchant of New Haven, Connecticut, who had gained notoriety for his participation in the capture of Fort Ticonderoga and Crown Point in April and May 1775.

For the assault on Quebec, Colonel Arnold chose to have his men conveyed by water to the mouth of the Kennebec, the ascent of which would be the shortest and most direct route to the St. Lawrence River and Quebec. Departing in transports north for Maine from Newburyport Massachusetts, Arnold's men spent the last few days of summer sailing past Sagadahoc, where the first English attempt to settle Maine occurred a century and a half earlier. Proceeding up the Kennebec past the confluence with the Androscoggin, they halted at Gardiner, where they exchanged transport ships for bateaux, large flat-bottomed boats with many oar-locks for rowing upriver and poles for pushing forward in shoal water. A few birch-bark canoes were employed, but mostly for reconnaissance.

The strong current of the Kennebec provided an exhausting impediment for men unaccustomed to rowing unwieldy boats up wild rivers. Ticonnick Falls and Skowhegan Falls demanded portage by land; the men were forced to carry and drag the boats, their supplies and weapons, on make-shift trails created by the swiftly swung ax. Just below Ticonnick Falls was the location of Fort Halifax, built in 1754 anticipating the French-Indian War to guard against Indian and French raiders using this most typical route from Quebec to the settlements on the Maine seacoast. Fort Halifax was at the confluence of the Kennebec and Sebasticook rivers; the site of the fort is found by today's intrepid traveler at Winslow, Maine. The upriver route from Fort Halifax to Fort Western was difficult to navigate. Arnold's men arrived at Fort Western on the first day of autumn, 1775. Fort Western was built in 1754 but was scarcely used after the French-Indian War. By the time of Arnold's expedition it was a fortified tavern, a way-station for the errant traveler. Today's visitor can tour the grounds of the Fort Western Museum at Augusta. It is at a delightful spot, an urban park, overlooking the Kennebec River.

Proceeding upriver from Fort Western, they abandoned sloops for the bateaux and set out for the upper reaches of the Kennebec. Private Abner Stocking, who kept a journal of his experiences under Colonel Arnold, wrote of the increasing fatigue of the journey, caused in part by the rapid shallow water that occasioned the men sometimes having to wade, pulling the boats from the bow and pushing from the stern. At Skowhegan Falls they had to drag the boats around a steep portage. On October 2nd they reached Norridgewock Falls, where once the Indian tribe of the same name lived. The remains of their settlement still existed; one or two hearty Maine frontiersmen occupied the site.

Upriver from Norridgewock about twenty miles Arnold's force departed the Kennebec for a shortcut to the Dead River. By the end of October, those soldiers who remained had ascended the Dead River to the watershed separating it from the Riviere Chaudiere in Canada, which would take them to Quebec. The region of the watershed was the most fatiguing and torturous for the men, who had little to eat, were sick, and exhausted. The planned assault on Quebec failed. By the time the remnant of Arnold's army arrived at the St. Lawrence River, it was decimated by hunger and fatigue. General Richard Montgomery's army arrived late, so that the assault had to be delayed until winter. The night of January 1, 1776, during a blizzard, the Americans tried to take Quebec; Montgomery was killed and Arnold wounded; hundreds of men were taken prisoner; Quebec did not fall.

Equally disastrous was the American assault on Castine three years later. Midway through the war, in June 1779, the inhabitants of Penobscot Bay were surprised by the presence of a British fleet transporting British redcoats to the peninsula of Castine in the bay. Ships of war guarded the disembarkment of 630 soldiers who began the construction of a fort. General Francis Maclean, the commander, hoped by this action to secure Nova Scotia from American attack as well as keep a constant supply of timber going to Nova Scotia shipyards. The government of Massachusetts, upon hearing the news, responded with its own flotilla of nineteen warships and three to four thousand militia, which set sail in July intent on dislodging the British from Castine, The Americans were able to make a landing and take a hill on the western side of the peninsula overlooking the British camp. From this high point the Americans assaulted the British with cannon, and it looked as if an easy victory would ultimately be achieved. British reinforcements, however, soon arrived, which put the American fleet on the defensive and indeed forced it to scatter with great loss of both men and equipment. Joseph Whipple, an acquaintance of Daniel Little, described the debacle:

A general chase, and unresisted destruction took place. Two of the American armed ships endeavored to get to sea by passing round Long-Island, which lies in the middle of the bay; but they were soon intercepted, the first being taken, and the other run ashore and blown up by her crew. The rest of their fleet, with the transports, fled in the utmost confusion to the head of the bay, and entered the mouth of Penobscot river. They were pursued by the British squadron, and after destroying the fleet at the head of navigation, landed in a wild, uncultivated country, on the western side of Penobscot river, without provisions or other necessaries, and had to explore their way through a pathless desert, for near a hundred miles, before they could reach a place where supplies were to be obtained. They travelled in detached parties, with Indian guides, and suffered every privation incident to a wilderness; their best provision was an occasional supply of the flesh of the Moose, roasted on the coals without any appendage. Exhausted with famine and fatigue, they at length gained the settled parts of the Kennebec river after having lost several men, who perished in the woods.[63]

Daniel Little had taken this route in 1774 during peacetime. He knew the struggles of such a wilderness flight as that of the American soldiers from Castine. Besides a few small towns and forts along the coast or at strategic locations up the most important rivers, most of Maine was a daunting wilderness. Maine was made known and settled slowly during the course of the eighteenth and nineteenth centuries due in part to the efforts of soldiers, surveyors, mapmakers, woodsmen, and missionaries who explored the upper reaches of Maine rivers to near their sources in the mountainous high-ground of central Maine and New Hampshire.

During this period of Revolution, there was a transformation in thought in America that was reflected in the life of Daniel Little. The pastor was not a theologian nor a political philosopher. He was a common-sense thinker. For him, the Revolution was an event requiring a practical response. In Maine, on the eastern frontier, what good did the British presence provide in terms of religion, agriculture, the economy, and morality? These were the top concerns of Daniel Little and his parishioners: how to make and live a good life according to the dictates of divine benevolence? Humans, jealous of power and wealth, frequently ignored the issues of peace, plenty, and piety that preoccupied Daniel Little. Conflict occurs, violence erupts, and often people

---

63 Whipple, 88.

question God's role in such disorder. Why does God countenance human suffering? Daniel Little, doubtless, asked this very question time and again, when he heard of the occupation of Boston, the destruction of neighboring Falmouth, and the British occupation of the Penobscot Valley in 1779. What were his friends and acquaintances, of Blue Hill, Castine, Deer Isle, and Mount Desert, formed five years earlier, experiencing? And for what reason? Little was not given to metaphysical subtleties, and one assumes that he spent little time worrying about the answers to such questions. What mattered to him were the basic beliefs that had brought him to the ministry in the first place: how can a person live a righteous life, even amid suffering and anxiety and pain? Thinking, then, that his job as shepherd of the parish was to help his parishioners with practical knowledge of divine and human affairs, Little met with people, counseled people, prayed with people, and taught people.

Eighteenth-century New England ministers were usually the most intelligent, best-informed people in the parish: Daniel Little was certainly considered so by the people of Kennebunk. His wisdom in prayer, his pious works to yield from the Creation the means of existence, his basic belief in the order of God's creation, which required respect toward all creatures, all humans, helped his parishioners through the dark times of war, uncertainty, want, and suffering. His interest in all matters faced by humans—civil, natural, moral, ecclesiastical—had resulted in the unexpected honor of a Master's degree in Arts, presented to him in 1766 by "the senatus academicus of Harvard college." Little had an inventive mind—though as with most humans, the reality of his accomplishments rarely equaled the ideas that begot his actions. Reputedly in 1770 he invented a sleigh, there having been no such device hitherto used by people on this eastern frontier. Elderly Kennebunk residents in the early nineteenth century recalled of Little that "he was always employed in devising some means for the promotion of the good of his parishioners. He took the lead in all measures suggested for this purpose, his opinions being entitled to great weight. He was much in the habit of visiting, and holding free and familiar conversation with his people, enquiring into all their worldly affairs, and advising with them as to the best method of managing their farms, their domestic concerns, and business of whatever character." It occurred to him during the third year of the war that the scarcity of metals useful in war could be remedied by an application of scientific principles to the making of steel. Little was known by his contemporaries as quite a chemist, no doubt because he had read extensively on the principle of phlogiston, a hypothetical combustible element found in certain substances. Little conceived of the idea of combining, in a heated furnace, certain substances that are high in phlogiston with bar iron. If the escape of phlogiston in the enclosed furnace could be effectively reduced, the molten bar iron would encompass a greater amount of the phlogiston. The problem was to find the substance with the most phlogiston that could provide, when combined with iron, a cementing effect on the iron, producing steel. He thought he had found the substance as he explored the Maine seacoast and picked up quantities of rockweed, a kind of seaweed that when washed and dried, then pulverized, and added to the iron, would infuse so much phlogiston into the iron as to make steel. This was the theory. The pastor made known to his parishioners his ideas on the subject. "All were anxious," people later recalled, "that the benefit of the discovery should not be lost by Mr. Little's inability to go on with the work." His parishioners recommended that he apply to the Massachusetts General Court for encouragement, which he did. The members of the General Court liked Little's ideas, and voted to fund his efforts with a grant of £450. The conditions were that Little "erect a building of thirty-five feet by twenty-five feet for the purpose of manufacturing steel; also, to build a furnace and convenient blacksmith's forge, and . . . to purchase utensils requisite for preparing and examining the [iron] bars." The legislature desired Little to "engage to carry the art of manufacturing steel to as great perfection as possible with the reach of the present knowledge, or any future acquirements, and to communicate the same without any reserve to the General Court of this State when they judge it will be most beneficial to the public." Little dutiful carried out the Court's instructions, but, as an early antiquarian put it, "the laws of nature were against him." Phlogiston was theory rather than fact. To make steel required carbon not seaweed. "Reluctantly, and much to his mortification, he was compelled to abandon his enterprise." If nothing else, Little achieved publication in the first issue of the *Memoirs* of the American Academy of Arts and Sciences, of which he was a member.[64]

In addition to Little's interest in phlogiston—essentially, eighteenth-century chemistry—he was, as were most of his

---

[64] Timothy Alden, *A Collection of American Epitaphs and Inscriptions* (New York: Marks, 1814), 107; Bourne, *History of Wells and Kennebunk*, 715-717; Daniel Little, "Observations upon the Art of making Steel," *Memoirs of the American Academy of Arts and Sciences*, 1(1783): 525-528

clerical brethren, interested in mineralogy, agriculture, and botany. Botany at this time was closely allied to medicine, as often the only person resembling a physician in the eighteenth century was the apothecary, that is, the expert on *materia medica* (the materials of medicine). In the scattered records of Little's life we find one that implies much about his interest in medicine. It appears that a parishioner had a cancerous growth on the body. Medical practitioners of Little's time—Europeans as well as American Indians—had a high regard to the application of poultices on skin lesions and swellings. Little learned and experimented with poultices sufficiently to advise his parishioner/patient to apply a poultice formed of clay on the cancerous growth. He published a paper on the experiment in the *Memoirs* of the American Academy of Arts and Sciences.[65]

Little wore quite comfortably the different hats of naturalist, inventor, scientist, clergyman, and missionary. The eighteenth-century clergyman was at the same time a naturalist and the eighteenth-century naturalist was typically given to piety. In an age when the truth of Scripture was not in doubt, when humans were clearly made in the image of God, when the Old Testament Law as modified by Christ was unquestioned, when God was yet the loving Creator whose Providence was pervasive, even the greatest minds could scarcely question the fundamental truths laid down by previous generations. There were Arminians and Deists to be sure, even the occasional atheist, but overall the minds produced by institutions of higher learning maintained an almost childlike awe of the Creator and the Creation. The

---

65   Bourne, *History of Wells and Kennebunk*, 718.

complexity and mystery of the Creation appeared throughout northern New England—the vast forests, the cascading streams, broad powerful rivers, and rocky seacoast. The most daunting natural phenomena were the White Mountains. Known by the native inhabitants long before the arrival of the Europeans as a forbidding place of mystery and danger, the first European explorers of the New England coast could spy the mountains, even from the sea, apparently glistening like crystal, according to Christopher Levett in 1624; John Smith referred to the highest as the "twinkling mountain." In time the English along the coast and further inland became convinced that there were gems, *carbuncles*, dotting the slopes. Indian legends made the mountains inaccessible, being a place haunted by nefarious spirits. The first explorers who ascended the highest, Agiocochook, what the English called the White Hill or Great Mountain—later Mount Washington—found not treasure but a forbidding landscape of snow and cold, even during summer months. The wind speed and power at the summit was astonishing. Here, reputedly, was awesome natural power; here was the beauty, grandeur, and immensity of God's Creation. The Great Mountain drew the treasure hunter, explorer, adventurer, scientist, and pious.

When precisely Daniel Little first felt the call of the White Mountains is not recorded. People of Newburyport and Haverhill, Massachusetts, Hampstead, Brentwood, and Portsmouth, New Hampshire, and York and Wells, Maine, knew the stories and legends of the White Mountains—a distant, daunting place. Little had doubtless seen the highest mountain at various times during his life. On clear days, Mount Washington can often be seen from coastal communities, even by mariners at sea. The first indication of Daniel Little's interest in visiting the mountains is found in a letter he wrote to his friend and fellow clergyman Jeremy Belknap in 1766. It was the second week in September, not particularly the best time to plan an expedition to one of the most dangerous peaks—Mount Washington—in North America. Nevertheless, Little wrote Belknap that he and unnamed others about Wells were planning just such a journey. "If the Expedition to the White Hills should be prosecuted this Season," Little wrote, "whatever occurs worthy of notice shall be communicated with pleasure." Plans were tentative, however. "If it should be postpon'd to another Season, you may expect to be advertised."[66]

The journey was postponed—for eighteen years. Why, precisely, it took so long for Little to realize his ambition to climb the Great Mountain, Agiocochook, is not entirely clear. In time, missionary activities in the early 1770s occupied his attention. Then, from 1775 to 1783, the danger of war made it inadvisable to journey far from settled communities. Wilderness trails connecting the Connecticut River with the rivers descending from the Great Mountain— the Saco, Ammonoosuc, Androscoggin, Pemigewasset— were strategically important, and at times under contention between British forces, usually their Indian allies, and local American militia. But with the signing of the Peace of Paris in 1783, the danger was removed. His enthusiasm for the journey had continued unabated, even though, in 1783, he was in his sixtieth year. Having heard of various recent journeys into the White Mountains, he wanted to go himself

---

66 Daniel Little to Jeremy Belknap, September 8, 1766, Belknap Papers, MHS.

while he still had his health.

Daniel Little's involvement in the New England natural science community ensured that he would hear the latest news respecting attempted ascents of the Great Mountain. In 1783, he learned from two brothers of the cloth, Rev. Joseph Haven of Rochester, New Hampshire, and William Fessenden of Fryeburg, Maine, that two men, Nehemiah Porter of Andover, Massachusetts, who owned land in Shelburne, New Hampshire, near the White Mountains, and a Mr. Ingalls of Shelburne, ascended the highest peak, the Great Mountain. They journeyed during the first week in September, apparently reached the summit, and although they were looking for precious metals, in particular silver, they came up empty-handed. This was the first attempted ascent since before the war. Little had previously heard (probably from his friend Jeremy Belknap) of the journey in October, 1774, of Nicholas Austin to the White Mountains. Austin had ascended the highest in pursuit of precious stones, but to no avail. He reported on his journey to the governor of the province, John Wentworth, who had himself journeyed to the White Mountains in 1772. Previously, Major Robert Rogers had attempted an ascent of the highest peak during the 1760s, but failed. Another soldier, a Captain Wells, had ascended the Great Mountain in 1725. And there had been earlier recorded ascents during the 1600s—by John Josselyn, Darby Field, Richard Vines, and Walter Neal. In all, there had been perhaps a half-a-dozen ascents of the Great Mountain, Mount Washington, since the English had established colonies in America. None of these journeys had as the ultimate purpose the acquisition of scientific knowledge. Such was the goal that drove Daniel Little and two other ministers, Jeremy Belknap and Manasseh Cutler, as well as land speculator Joseph Whipple, physician Joshua Fisher, and hunter, guide, and road-builder Captain John Evans, to penetrate the White Mountain wilderness in pursuit of climbing the highest peak in New England, Mount Washington.[67]

In June, 1784, Daniel Little wrote his friend Jeremy Belknap: "I wish to be informed seasonably of the Day you have fixed upon to be at Pigwacket on your Way to the White Hills." Belknap, like Little having longed to journey to the White Mountains, had arranged for the expedition, involving at least himself, Little, the guide John Evans, and Joseph Whipple of Portsmouth. Pigwacket, or Fryeburg, on the Saco River, was the home of John Evans, whom Belknap had fixed upon as their "pilot" for this adventure. Evans, Belknap had learned, had journeyed up the Great Mountain in 1774; his experience would be essential to guarantee a safe trip. Little had, unbeknown to Belknap, also recruited a few other journeyers: "also Wish," he wrote Belknap, "it may be Convenient to give the Same Information to Mr. [Manasseh] Cutler of Ipswich from whom I received a Line yesterday desiring me to accompany him there ab[ou]t middle of July if he succeeded in his Plan—his principle object is Botany."[68]

Little was concerned about his health, and his strength and stamina in so arduous an undertaking. He wished

---

67 Russell M. Lawson, *Passaconaway's Realm: Captain John Evans and the Exploration of Mountain Washington* (Hanover, NH: University Press of New England, 2004), 24, 40-41, 58-59, 65-66.

68 Daniel Little to Jeremy Belknap, June 1784, Belknap Papers, MHS.

Belknap to contrive the journey such that there might be several options available for climbers on the day of the climb: "The Mountains are large enough," Little wrote cryptically, "to employ our Time well without Interference but I wish the Plan may be so formed and the Time so prefixed that there may be Junction at the opening of the Scene at the foot of the Mountains or at best between the two Proposition[s] to me [that] I may not be disappointed and left in the Rear. I am serious in my Intentions," he went on, "about the Matter think it a laudable and Useful Design and hope it will be well conducted. Nothing but my want of Health to bear so long a Ride at so hot a Season will prevent my joining."[69]

Although Little's letter implied that he would journey directly to Fryeburg, there to rendezvous with Belknap and the others, he changed his plans and decided to journey south to the Piscataqua valley and proceed to Belknap's home in Dover. What route Little took is lost to time: perhaps he journeyed directly south to Kittery, crossed the Piscataqua by ferry, and journeyed upriver by boat or on horseback to Bloody Point, where he could cross by ferry to Dover Point, and proceed to the Belknap parsonage. Another possibility is that Little journeyed west-southwest toward Berwick, along what is today Route 9, to reach the falls of the Cocheco River. Notwithstanding his path, he arrived in the third week of July and was ready when he, Belknap, Cutler, Fisher, Whipple, and three other men set forth, north, toward the White Mountains. Daniel Little kept a journal of his adventure, which does not begin until July 23rd, when the

---

69 Ibid.

men had journeyed north of Dover to Rochester, Wakefield, and Ossipee to Conway, New Hampshire, where they rendezvoused with their guide, John Evans, at the tavern of Andrew McMillan. McMillan and Evans were veterans of the French-Indian War, as such receiving grants of land along the upper Saco River.[70]

From McMillan's, the men followed their guide Captain Evans, journeying by horseback, paralleling the Saco two miles to its confluence with the Ellis River, which they followed along a make-shift trail euphemistically called the Shelburne Road. Little reported that the men "set off to the great Mountain 8 ½ o'clock in the morning," arriving "at the foot of the Mountains . . . about 4 o'clock, in season to make a good camp near a meadow," from which they could perceive the sources of two rivers, the Ellis, flowing south to the Saco, and the Peabody, flowing north to the Androscoggin. After a restless night attempting to sleep in a makeshift hut of pine boughs constructed by Captain Evans, the men set forth up the eastern slopes of the Great Mountain, Mount Washington, at 6:30 a.m. on July 24th. After climbing for a short time, Dr. Fisher and Rev. Belknap, the former being in "poor health" and the latter "being very corpolant [sic]," returned to camp, leaving the remaining eight men to make the ascent. Little kept precise time: the ascent lasted "6 hours and 51 minutes"; "our stops for resting were short and frequent 3, 4, and 5 minutes at a time, in the

---

70 The details of this journey are found in a number of sources, in particular the journals and letters of Belknap, Cutler, and Little, all of which are summarized in Lawson, *Passaconaway's Realm*.

whole 1 hour and 30 minutes."[71]

Today there are a variety of means to ascend Mount Washington: by automobile on the Mount Washington Auto Road; by means of the Mount Washington Cog Railway on the western slope of the mountain; or a half-dozen well-marked trails of varying difficulty. For years the Appalachian Mountain Club has maintained trails and huts to accommodate the hiker. Upon reaching the summit, there is the Mount Washington Observatory, a weather station occupied year-round. Obviously, the mountain was quite different in 1784. Only half a dozen ascents had been made previously, and these explorers had not left behind trail markers and clear paths for other journeyers. There were animal traces that the men could take, and streams falling from the summit to mark the way up and down.

Captain Evans led the hikers up the eastern slope paralleling a descending stream christened a few years before as New River. "The first two thirds of the mountain," Little wrote, was "covered with thick growth of wood, chiefly spruce & fir, the last mile of which they shorten gradually till they terminate in a short moss and grass for a few rods," perhaps thirty to thirty-five feet. These dwarf evergreens were called *krummholz*, and impeded the men's steps significantly. Whereupon "vegetation is almost at an end, and the grand ascen[t] up the naked rocky part of the mountain begins. This ascent is like steep stairs, the rocks different forms, wedged in by one another in various altitudes and bigness." The climb here, nearing the summit,

---

71 *Mr. Little's Tour of the White Mountains*, typescript, Brick Store Museum, Kennebunk, Maine, 1.

was treacherous and fatiguing, requiring "our utmost exertions" for almost an hour. The initial summit was "a spacious plain, roughly paved with stones of pretty equal bigness, on which we walked about half a mile to the base of the Sugar Loaf," the final summit, so-called by the first explorers during the previous century. The final ascent was "300 feet perpendicular from its base." On the summit, the force of the wind is most extreme, making the hottest summer day feel like winter. "Here, here, is a grand prospect! The heavens clear upon our first arrival. The houses on the Connecticut River" to the west "open to view with the naked eye." The paths of other rivers flowing from the White Mountains were evident. "Numerous large mountains on every side, but the N. Westerly sometimes appearing in rays of a very clear sun, and very soon shut up from sight by the ascending vapor and thickening clouds, then appearing again. This diversity of scenery closed in a thick fog, and as cold as November." Little tried to use a hammer and chisel to carve the letters *NH* into a rock, but his hands were so cold that he had to give it up. The icy fog so enveloped the men that they were in danger of losing their bearings; the men grew frightened and requested that Captain Evans lead them on a quick descent, which they accomplished, though with great difficulty and danger, reaching the tree line, where they made camp.[72]

After a night spent under a makeshift pine hut on the eastern side of Mount Washington, Captain Evans led the men back to camp, where they found Dr. Fisher and Rev. Belknap. Thereupon they pursued the trail north, leaving the

---

72 Ibid, 1-2.

Eastern, or Pinkham, Notch, paralleling a tributary of the Androscoggin River, the Peabody River. "Set off ½ past 9 o'clock," Little recorded, "to surround the mountain, with a design to return to Conway by the Western branch of the Saco River, which proceeds from the mountains at their Western side." The Saco River rises from the western slopes of Mount Washington at what Little and his contemporaries called the Western Notch, today known as Crawford Notch. "Rode about 6 miles," Little continued, "from our camp on the road that leads to Shelburn[e], then took the road that leads from Shelburn[e] on Androscoggin River to upper Cohoss," on the Connecticut River. "Travelled about northwest till night came on, and then camped till morning." July 26th, the men continued their journey west toward Dartmouth (Jefferson), a small town or plantation governed by the owner Colonel Joseph Whipple. Whipple resided in Portsmouth, but spent summers on his plantation. Dartmouth was "28 miles from our first encampment, which we expected to accomplish in a day, but the road being unimproved for 7 years the windfalls and bushes made it slow riding. Whipple's plantation was situated on the Israel River, like all the rivers in this mountainous country shallow and cold, flowing through fertile forested land featuring "large and tall, black birch, ash, rock maple, chiefly."[73]

As Little was wont to do with such people so far removed from settled religion, he gathered the farmers, *servants* to Whipple, thirty-eight in all, in a large barn, where they heard a sermon preached by Rev. Belknap; Little baptized eight children. There was no settled church here, yet there was the

---

73 Ibid., 2-3.

sublimity of the Creation. Sometimes when a person cannot put much faith in human institutions, either because of neglect, or war, or poverty, one must turn to *Elder Scripture*, the continuity, sameness, beauty, and wonder of nature, where God's love is surely found. The travelers experienced this directly, as they departed Whipple's for the Western Notch, "a place grand and curious, where the Creator has marked a central road thro[ugh] an extensive and fertile country to the province of Canada." The notch was a narrow defile between huge mountainous walls, the one to the east the slopes of the Great Mountain, surrounded by numerous peaks, subsequently called the Presidentials, named for such leaders as Adams, Jefferson, Madison, Monroe, Jackson, and Eisenhower. The state of New Hampshire had commenced work on a road through this notch so "to widen the passage sufficient for the water and the road." The road would be able to host wagon traffic, "thro[ugh] which the wealth of our extensive & fertile country may be easily conveyed to market," connecting the Connecticut River settlements (called the Cohos) with the towns of the Piscataqua valley and the eastern frontier of Maine.[74]

From the Western Notch, the journeyers paralleled the descending Saco River back to Conway, from which, after staying the night at McMillan's, they departed, Belknap joining Little east along the Saco into Maine, while the others departed south toward Rochester and Dover. Belknap, who was working on an extensive history of New Hampshire, wished to visit Lovewell's Pond at Fryeburg, the site of a battle between Massachusetts militia and Pequawket

---

74 Ibid., 3.

Indians in 1725. Little accompanied him as they toured the pond, examining the remnants of the fight, such as the marks of musket balls in the surrounding trees. Belknap and Little stayed with Captain Henry Brown, one of the proprietors of the lands in the upper Saco valley. They continued their journey very early on the morning of July 30th, paralleling the Saco River to the Great Falls, which the two scientists observed, were "not more than 40 feet perpendicular, though the descent may be as many rods." They learned that rocks prevented salmon from ascending above the falls; rather the fish swam up the "Great Ossapy River, on which is the remains of an Indian weir, built with stones and wood, for taking them." They crossed the Ossipee River above its confluence with the Saco; "our horses swam after a canoe, in which we put our saddles and bags; an old woman paddled us over." From here they continued south to a small town, Limerick. "In the evening got to Massabesick [Waterboro]; crossed Little Ossapy on a bridge. Lodged at Captain Smith's." Captain John Smith was one of the original settlers of Waterboro; his house was a town focal point. Little and Belknap had journeyed forty-seven miles from McMillan's Tavern.[75]

At Massabesick, Little and Belknap separated, the latter riding southwest to New Hampshire while Little rode another sixteen miles to Kennebunk. During his solitary journey, Little noted "the improvements . . . were great, and

---

[75] Jeremy Belknap, "Tour to the White Mountains," Belknap Papers, *Collections of the Massachusetts Historical Society*, Series 5, Volume 2 (Boston: Massachusetts Historical Society, 1877), 396-401; Willis Lord, *History of Waterboro*,1987:http://www.waterboro-me.net/docs/information/history_waterboro.html

the wheat extraordinary, both summer and winter [varieties], and all kinds of produce promised a joyful harvest." He was filled with thanks. The mountains, said John Josselyn, are "daunting terrible," and most of the native inhabitants as well as the English colonists agreed. They were dangerous meteorologically, because of the wind and cold, but also, reportedly, spiritually—at least the local inhabitants had convinced themselves that evil spirits reigned among these forbidding peaks. Little, not given to such nonsense, said simply: "Through the care of Heaven in this tour, man and beast have been surprizingly preserved from harm; for which may the praise be given where it is due."[76]

Such was Daniel Little's philosophy during the years of conflict, anguish, foreboding, and suffering that was the American Revolution. Little was a practical rather than metaphysical thinker. To him, Christianity was not complex: it involved accepting the love of God and responding to others in the spirit of said love. He refused to be bogged down in the religious subtleties of his age, and assumed during the war years that God's love extended to everyone: friend, enemy, English, Indian. The Church of England, the official church led by the King and Archbishop of Canterbury, was dominated by words and liturgy and ceremony. The Bible, Baptism, and Lord's Supper were sufficient for Little. He felt no duty toward the Archbishop, much less the King, nor any prelate or religious leader—only Christ. Little's practicality had led him toward the Patriot side. The eastern frontier had been settled by British-Americans, and there was no reason for these people to give

---

76 *Little's Tour of the White Mountains*, 4.

up their rights or liberties to lords and monarchs. Likewise, he reasoned, the original inhabitants of the land should receive the blessings due them—blessings such as the right to listen to and read the words of the Bible. Unlike some clergy, Little was not political. Always before him was the message to bring to those who had yet heard it. In the years after the war, rather than engaging himself in the nuances of politics, he engaged himself in the Great Commission. There was much yet to do, many journeys yet to take.

5 THE HIGHEST PEAK

Mount Katahdin in Maine, at 5,267 feet, is the highest mountain in Maine. It lies at the end of the Appalachian chain, and is one of the most dramatic peaks among American mountains. Katahdin juts out of the forest, a rocky crag soaring skyward. This solitary peak is made even more isolated by its distance from eastern settlements--it stands near the source of the Penobscot River. The native Abenakis referred to it as the *highest peak*, Teddon, and generally feared to ascend it as being the home of evil spirits from which the climber would not return. Captain John Gyles in the late seventeenth century heard from the Abenakis that one Indian warrior tried the ascent only to lose his senses in the process. They also told Gyles that it is a mountain greater in height than Agiocochook, the Great White Hill of New Hampshire (Mount Washington). Ninety years later the scientist and clergyman Daniel Little of Kennebunk journeyed up the Penobscot River to the region approaching Katahdin, where the white settlers and native inhabitants spoke in awe of Teddon. The legend of Katahdin, the unconquerable mountain, higher than any others in America, equal to the highest peaks in the world, was not dispelled until scientists journeyed to the lofty peak and vanquished the specters of fantasy and myth.

During the autumn of 1784 and winter and spring of 1785, Daniel Little, Jeremy Belknap, Manasseh Cutler, and Joseph Whipple continued their conversations, in person and by letter, about their journey to the White Mountains. Little traveled south to Boston during the winter, sometimes staying at Cutler's in Hamilton, Massachusetts, and preaching for him. On one visit to Belknap's at Dover, Little said that the experience of journeying to Mount Washington was so exhilarating that it caused the journeyers to be "married for life." They discussed a return journey, and all that they wanted to discover. They engaged in scientific commentary on their discoveries. For much of the journey, the weather had been cloudy, preventing "our making such use of our glasses," as Little called telescopes, "as was to be wished." During their brief time at the base and on the summit of the Great Mountain, Manasseh Cutler, the most scientific of the men, used his barometer to make measurements, hoping to determine the altitude according to ranges in barometric pressure. He optimistically assumed that the Great Mountain was one of the highest in the world—certainly the highest in North America—at around nine thousand feet above sea level. The men took temperature readings, and determined that July on the Great Mountain was similar to November and March on the New England coastline. The base of the Great Mountain (and surrounding summits, from the Eastern to the Western notches), they estimated to be a circumference of forty miles. A concern among scientists at the time was the source of the whiteness of the White Mountains: is it snow? the soil? the rocks? the grasses? "The rocks on the upper part of the mountain," Little reported, "are in general a dark grey, in some places are veins and spots of white flint, they are covered with a hard short scaly moss of a dark grey colour." The sun shining upon white flint and gray rocks, often snow-covered, accounts for the whiteness. "Springs of water," he continued, "are on every degree of ascent till you ascend the

Sugar Loaf." The waters descending from the mountain were extensive, enough to account for the great rivers sprung thereupon.[77]

Daniel Little was not to return to the White Mountains, in part because he turned once again to the eastern frontier. Belknap, in one letter to Cutler, told his friend that "Father Little" thinks the "Penobscot as superior. His heart is much set on the Eastern Country."[78] Indeed, Little could not help but journey there again and again. During his 1785 journey, his third trip to the eastern frontier, he combined missionary work and scientific research in the Penobscot Valley. Inspired by his journey the year before to Mount Washington, Little yearned to find out what he could about Katahdin—perhaps he secretly hoped to advance far enough up the Penobscot to approach it. Excited by his experience in the White Mountains, which changed his life because of its combination of adventure, research, and missionary work, he enthusiastically, the following June, set forth from Kennebunk on the trail once again to the Penobscot valley. He would be absent from home for more than two months.

Little recalled in 1788 that in "the year 1785, at a periodical Meeting of Ministers at Dr. [Benjamin] Stevens in Kittery I suggested to my Brethren the high probability, that the ravages of the British Army had impoverished and distressed those infant plantations and that they had been without religious instruction in the days of their trouble, and therefore I wished, if my pulpit could be Supplyed [sic], to make them another Visit. The motion was agreeable to my

---

77 *Ibid*, 3-4; Cutler, *Life*, 2: 224.

78 Cutler, *Life*, 2: 242.

worthy Brethren, eleven of whom offered to Supply my Pulpit, my own People giving one day, which gift of Service by 12 Ch[urc]hs I found very Seasonable and acceptable to the people." Daniel Little continued to travel under the auspices of the General Court of Massachusetts. Although Little kept a journal of his experiences and observations, the journal was at some point lost to posterity, only a few parts of it surviving in transcriptions of his journey and observations he made about the native peoples that he provided for Jeremy Belknap, along with a letter to Belknap, and others to Benjamin Stevens and Isaac Smith. The records of his Kennebunk parish note only that "June 20. Mr. Little set out on a 3d mission to Penobscot."[79]

Whether Little traveled by land or boat to and from Kennebunk in 1785 is unknown, though it is probable that Little went by land to the Penobscot, as he arrived at the same place—Rockport and Camden on the western shores of Penobscot Bay—from which he had departed eleven years ago at the end of his 1774 missionary journey. In 1774, Little had held a service of baptism for a family living on the Megunticook River, and had stayed at Major William Minot's home. This 1785 journey, he noted particularly the remarkable in the landscape and vegetation that he observed. "Passing thro[ugh] Camden adjoining the Penobscot Bay in the Month of June," Little recalled, "I observed a Young Growth of Oak and Maples for Several Acres together which had the Appearance of Trees killed by a ruinous fire but upon Examination found it was occasioned by Worms who were

---

79 Little, "General Account of the Rise and Progress of the Eastern Mission;"; *Records of the First Parish Church.*

just finishing their Harvest. The People say they are hatched from the Eggs of a Caterpillar which are laid on the Smooth Bark of trees in the Month of Sep[tembe]r to which they adhere and are hatched by the Heat of the Sun. The May following they are one Inch in length of a dark brown Colour. The Leaves of other Trees adjoining and intermixed, remain untouched in full Verdure."[80]

During the next week Little journeyed, no doubt by canoe, rowboat, or schooner, across westernmost Penobscot Bay past Isleboro, which perchance he visited, as he had in 1772 and 1774—he might have even revisited his stay with Captain Jonathan Parker. From here he crossed to the northeast, arriving during the first week of July at the Bagaduce River (still called by Little Majabeguceduce River). The northern head of land at the mouth of the river, Castine, was where so much of the drama of 1779 had played out: the British occupation of the site, choosing it as an apt headquarters for their colony of New Ireland; the fortification of Fort George; the American naval attack and subsequent defeat; the continued British occupation of the site until the end of the war. Nature does not often bend to human conflict. Little discovered this as he surveyed the crops in the Bagaduce valley: "Barley in full ear. Garden Peas, the largest Pods 2 ¾ Inches in length."[81]

From Bagaduce, Little journeyed south and east on quite a significant journey toward Mount Desert Island; he passed

---

80 "Minutes of the Progressive Growth and Maturity of the most useful Vegetables at Penobscot &c. with Some recreational observations in the year 1785 by the Rev[eren]d Mr. Little, while Missionary there," Belknap Papers, MHS.

81 Ibid.

Deer Isle, sailed past Naskeag Point, then wound through the Mount Desert Narrows to "Penobscot River No. 1," today the town of Trenton, where, on July 10th, Little found "fine Flax in full Blossom—The first Mowing of their best Clover Grass." Little had passed by Number One on his 1774 journey, and perhaps he had visited the place two years previously in 1772. After having made this long journey through the peninsula between the Union and Jordan rivers, he proceeded quickly on to Frenchman's Bay, then made a hasty departure and return through the Mount Desert Narrows, past Naskeag Point and Deer Isle, into the western bay and "30 miles up" the Penobscot River, arriving at this unknown location on July 16th. Here the grass--perhaps at Sowadabscook, modern Hampden—was "in full Blossom and the "Flowers of red Clover dried." Two days later Little had ascended the river another half-dozen miles to the head of tide, which he called Pleasant Point, today's Bangor. Here, at "the uppermost English Settlement," Little observed Indian Corn, the leaves extended 4 feet 5 Inches"; the "Bean Pods" were "2 Inches long." He noted in his journal that "the farther we ascend this River the more fertile the Soil."[82]

    Little stopped at Pleasant Point on his way to Old Town, a Penobscot town situated on an island in the Penobscot found ten miles above Pleasant Point. Little had hitherto not journeyed this far up the Penobscot. He arrived on July 18th, and spent two days among the Penobscot people. He described Old Town as "ten miles above the Head of the Tide" and "70 miles north from the Entrance of Penobscot Bay at the Fox Island, or Owls Head." Old Town, Little

---

82 Ibid.

wrote, is "on an island in the River on the lower Point of which stand the Indian Houses in 2 Ranges, in very exact Order, of the Same Dimensions and Materials, around which they plant their Corn &c, the longest leaves of which extended 4 Feet and 10 Inches. The Spindle visisible [sic] 4 Inches and the Shoots for ear the Same. Their Manure [is] Alewives, of which they cover with Earth around the hills, at planting—the soil high Intervale."[83]

For Little to journey above the limits of English settlement to an Indian village, and to stay there for several days observing, conversing, and learning, reveals not only courage but commitment, an indefatigable desire to bring the Scriptures to people who were ignorant of Christianity—that is, Protestant Christianity. Very few English had come this way, especially since 1764, when a party of English explorers journeyed up the Penobscot to Old Town, from which they departed for the upper reaches of the Penobscot, and the legendary mountain, Katahdin.

At the close of the French-Indian War the victorious English had taken control of Canada and were involved in the daunting prospect of governing the Catholic French and the many Indian tribes that were former French allies. The task of governing such a vast empire of inhabitants recently at war and of such disparity in culture and religion demanded from the English bold and imaginative plans. It was obvious to the English that stable communications were absolutely necessary. Good roads, connecting the thirteen British colonies with Quebec, had to be constructed. Only then could the hinterland be settled, the wilderness conquered,

---

[83] Ibid.

and a stable empire be created. The government of Massachusetts was interested in building a road through the northern wilderness to connect the Penobscot region (Fort Pownall) with Quebec. Massachusetts Governor Francis Bernard appointed James Chadwick to survey the area in preparation for building such a path or road. Already British surveyor Colonel John Montresor had journeyed from Quebec to Topsham, Maine, and back during the winter of 1759-1760, surveying and mapping the region from Quebec to the Kennebec and Penobscot. His map of the region was published in 1761.[84]

The Massachusetts expedition of 1764 was commanded by Captain John Preble, who would guide Daniel Little up the Penobscot River in 1774; Preble was the son of Jedidiah, with whom Little briefly served during the French-Indian War. John Preble guided surveyors James Chadwick and William Crawford, who was also a surgeon, justice of the peace, and chaplain at Fort Pownall. James Chadwick kept a journal of the expedition. The Penobscot and other tribes were reluctant to allow the English into the region of the headwaters of the Penobscot River. Chadwick noted that the jealousy of the Indians made the chief goals of the expedition, to survey and map the land, difficult. The English wisely hired eight Indians, including the Penobscot sachem Joseph Aspegueunt, to guide the expedition. But, even then, the natives were not satisfied.[85]

---

[84] Fannie Hardy Eckstorm, "History of the Chadwick Survey from Fort Pownal in the District of Maine to the Province of Quebec in Canada in 1764," *Sprague's Journal of Main History* 14(1926): 63-89.

[85] Ibid., 75.

The expedition set out in May 1764 from Fort Pownall, ascending the river about six miles by birch-bark canoe to Salmon Point, near Bucksport on the eastern shores of the Penobscot, from which they journeyed a dozen miles up the Penobscot to the confluence of the Sowadabscook with the Penobscot, modern Hampden. The following day they reached Old Town on Penobscot Island, having had to find portage around Treat's Falls. Old Town was for centuries the central location for the Tarrantine then the Penobscot Indians. Here the English explorers and the local Penobscots had a disagreement about the purposes of the journey and how far up the river the English should be allowed to go. Chadwick implied that the disagreement came close to turning ugly. At last the two parties reached a deal whereby the surveyors would be restricted from mapmaking--only journal entries would be allowed. The Indians told Chadwick that when they were "amongst English Men thay obayed [sic] their Commands & now best way you do obay Indeins [sic] Orders."[86]

As the expedition was to proceed as quickly as possible, Chadwick and Crawford were not to employ surveying chains, rather to use a method of estimating distance from the daily travels of their birch-bark canoes, what mariner's called *dead reckoning*. Governor Bernard had ordered Chadwick to mark a place on the Penobscot (at Treat's Falls just below Old Town) beyond which settlers should limit their beaver trapping. The Indians had requested of the Governor a limit on English settlement into the interior as their beaver supply was slowly diminishing. They claimed

---

[86] Ibid., 73

that their practice in hunting was to trap 2/3^{rds} of beaver every third year but leave 1/3rd to breed. But the English took beaver without limit, guaranteeing less beaver in the future. Indians also claimed to allot various lands for hunting to various tribes and individuals.[87]

Old Town had about fifty families living in a long house of dimensions 50 by 20 feet made of birch bark walls and spruce bark for the roof. When Little visited Old Town there were two of these long houses, indicating a growing population. In 1764, Chadwick saw the remains of the French-Catholic parish church destroyed by the English in 1723 during Dummer's War. Proceeding upriver seven miles the expedition came to a large breadth in the river, like a bay with many islands. There was evidence of frequent flooding (what settlers called a *freshet*). The Indians grew maize and made maple sugar, but relied mostly on fishing and trapping for their sustenance. The surrounding forest was of maple, oak, birch, and white pine mast trees. Distant mountains to the north appeared blue. These Indians were Catholic, and had once traveled to Quebec for marriage and baptism. Since the end of the French-Indian War, however, the English control of Quebec meant a declining emphasis on Catholicism. In response, the Indians invited Preble, Chadwick, and Crawford to a ceremony in a wigwam; the chiefs were finely dressed and all sat on beaver pelts. The leaders presented speeches requesting that the English supply a Catholic missionary to live among them; otherwise they would forget the faith. The explorers gave little encouragement that the petition would receive a favorable

---

[87] Ibid., 77.

response.[88]

From here the explorers turned northwest along the Piscataquis River to Sebec Stream then Sebec Lake, then on to Lake Onawa, following a course of streams used by the Indians for ages. They used Boarstone (Bearston) Mountain for bearings. Chadwick described Moosehead Lake and the Moose Hills, called such from an old Indian legend. Today Moose Hills are part of the range of Longfellow Mountains. Here was the watershed over which the land descended toward the St. Lawrence. The expedition apparently proceeded along the North Branch of the Penobscot River into Canada, where they found their way to the Riviere Chaudiere and Quebec.[89]

In his journal Chadwick discussed the Indian trail to the upper Connecticut and the Cohos of New Hampshire. Hunters and Indians informed him of the best path from Penobscot to Quebec for the building of a road. In Quebec, some of his informants were St. Francis Indians. In the region of the Chaudiere River in Quebec were the sources of the Kennebec, Penobscot, and Connecticut rivers. Chadwick noted that the St. John's River, the source of which is also in the region of northwest Maine near the Canadian border, is the most direct route to the sea because of fewer obstructions.

On the return journey, the explorers traveled from Moosehead Lake to Chesuncook Lake, which was in the mid-eighteenth century much smaller than it is today (because of Ripogenus Dam); the lake was shallow and

---

[88] Ibid.

[89] Ibid., 80-81.

muddy with grassy, tree-lined banks. The West Branch of the Penobscot took them near Mount Katahdin, today's Baxter State Park. Chadwick for unknown reasons spurned the Indian word for the mountain, referring to it as Satinhungemoss Hill, which "Lays in the Latitude of 45' 43" and from Fort Pownall 184 miles as we travel[e]d and 116 miles by Computation." Chadwick wrote further that the "Indians say that this Hill is the hightest in the Country. That thay can ascend as high as any Greens Grow & no higher. That one Indine attempted to go higher but he never returned."[90]

From the Katahdin region, they descended the Penobscot to Mattawamkeag, an Indian town at the confluence of the Penobscot with Mattawamkeag River. This was an old Indian town for military operations, mostly deserted when Chadwick saw it. A few inhabitants maintained the old Catholic parish church, its books, linens, and plate, as well as an old bell that still rang for mass. Local hunters told Chadwick that the fertile land, which hosted much Indian corn, became to the east a massive spruce swamp. The eastern branch of the Mattawamkeag, Chadwick learned, flows into the St. Croix River.[91]

Whether or not Daniel Little knew of James Chadwick's journey, Little's visit to Old Town and conversations with the Penobscots put him in mind of the upper Penobscot and the forbidding peak of Tadden. During his two-day stay at Old Town, he learned from the Indians the essentials of Katahdin, and enough information on the river pathways to

---

[90] Ibid., 83-84.

[91] Ibid., 82.

the mountain as to draw a remarkably accurate map, based entirely on oral communication. Little's map, "Plan of the Penobscot River from the H[ea]d of the Tide to the H[eigh]t of Land taken from the Indians July 18 1786," is hand drawn. From top to bottom, he draws the Penobscot and its tributaries in the "H[eigh]t of Land" to the northwest of "Taddon" and "Cross Pond" to the northeast. Between two branches of the Penobscot he situates Katahdin, drawn as forested up to its bald pinnacle: "Taddon is the highest the Indians say, above the White Mountains, and naked top[p]ed like them." Like Chadwick, Little correctly showed south of Katahdin the confluence of the Mattawamkeag River, which he wrote as "R. Montawamkeag," with the Penobscot. Below this confluence, Little correctly showed the confluence of the East Penobscot Branch with the main river; Little referred to the East Branch as "Mitishaton," a possible transliteration for Matagamon, a lake that is one of the sources of the East Branch. Further south, Little noted a widening of the Penobscot, with islands, east of which was the river Papaduskee [Passadumkeag], west of which was the river Passquattequness [Piscataquis]. This widening was "30 miles above H[ead] of Tide." The broad river south soon broke into different channels caused by other tributaries, which formed the island of Old Town, which on Little's map he puts at "12 miles from the head of Tide." South of Old Town, near what is today Orono, Little drew half a dozen houses, indicating the "uppermost English Settlement." Just below Little drew a town, denoting Pleasant Point, or Bangor, stating that "this head of the Tide 60 miles" from the mouth of the Penobscot.[92]

The survival of Little's map is due to the archival tendencies of his friend Belknap, to whom Little sent a draft of the map. Belknap wrote Cutler of Little's "plan of the upper part of Penobscot River, in one crotch of which is a mountain, which the Indians called Tadden, i. e., the highest, and say it is bald-pated like our Saconian [White] Mountains, and exceeds them in altitude. Asking their pardon," Belknap joked, "I think them very poor judges, as it is well known they have no mode of mensuration, and are afraid to ascend high mountains, lest they should invade the Territory of Hobomocko."[93] Hobomock, Belknap had learned from his research in history, was the evil spirit of some Algonquian tribes. Legends of the White Mountains indicated that Passaconaway haunted Agiocochook. The Abenakis of Maine, according to Fannie Hardy Eckstorm, likewise believed that Katahdin was haunted, in particular by Pamola, "the spirit of the night wind." To some, Pamola "harmed only those who would ascend the upper slopes of the mountain." In another version of the legend Pamola was "a storm bird that lived on Katahdin and flew about snatching up a child or a moose." Other stories pictured Pamola as a giant who lived on Katahdin, his thunderous

---

92 "Plan of the Penobscot River from the H[ea]d of the Tide to the H[eigh]t of Land taken from the Indians July 18 1786," Belknap Papers, MHS. Jeremy Belknap wrote Manasseh Cutler in November, 1785, that Daniel Little had sent a draft of this "Plan" to the Penobscot River shortly after his return from his 1785 journey.

93 Cutler, *Life*, 2: 235.

ways heard for miles around.[94]

After this brief yet memorable visit, Little departed Indian Old Town and returned down the Penobscot to Bagaduce. Here he stayed, it appears, for about a fortnight, making investigations and, no doubt, serving the religious needs of the local inhabitants. On July 20th, he reported that the "Wheat is in blossom; Green Peas in Plenty; Currants ripe; great Crops of english Hay, now in the height of Harvest." On the 24th he noted, "Potatoes in full Blossom the Roots 3 Inches in Circumference." During the last week in July, Little was on the move again, south past Deer Isle to Naskeag Point, northeast through the Mount Desert Narrows north of Mount Desert, on to Frenchman's Bay, perhaps as far as Flanders Bay and Gouldsboro. Along the way he observed at Naskeag Point "the first reaping of the best Fields of Winter Rye." By the second week in August, he had arrived at Blue Hill, writing from there to Rev. Benjamin Stevens that "I have extended my Services as far eastward as Frenchman's bay, and am now on my Return thro' the Islands homeward." He had spent the most recent Sabbath among the people of Blue Hill, the parish of "which I gathered in ye year [17]72." Here, amid visits and church business, Little feasted on "2 Ears of ro[a]sted corn, 8 Inches in length 5 Inches in Circumference, planted the 21 May, on a Gravelly Soil the Manure Barn dung and kelp," seaweed. "Flax in gen[era]l good and ripe, some Fields pulled. Winter Rye harvest completed." Harvest time for these farm people was of utmost importance. Little joined in on the

---

94 Eckstorm is quoted in Gorham B. Munson, *Penobscot: Down East Paradise* (Philadelphia: Lippincott, 1959).

conversations: "The Reapers this Day began their Wheat Harvest—Summer Wheat—they had their Seed 10 Years ago from Quebeck, and it has escaped the Mildew ever Since; tho' their Fields lie open to Mount Desert Bay, and exposed to the Air and Fogs from the Sea, they have 15-20 Bushels for Bushel Increase; they had tried the Siberian Wheat which Mildewed the 3^d Year—how then is the Changes of Seed a Security against the Mildew as it is often said?"[95]

The parish at Blue Hill was one of Little's success stories. "They have remarkably preserved good order," he wrote Dr. Stevens, "& Christian fellowship over time, tho' without a stated Pastor." Little participated in an orderly Sabbath during which "they had 20 members of their Communion beside Strangers." Unlike some of the peoples on the eastern frontier, the inhabitants of Blue Hill had resisted itinerant preachers preaching a message of emotion and enthusiasm. Little's presence on the eastern frontier was to combat such sentiments. "In almost every Place there are evident marks of an hopeful religious Concern upon ye minds of many whose particular & various Circumstances have taken up much of my time in private Conversation I hope with some happy fruits." Even here in the far

---

95 "Minutes of the Progressive Growth and Maturity"; "Copy of a Letter from Rev. Mr. Little of Wells to Rev. Dr. Stevens," August 15, 1785, Belknap Papers, MHS. Eight years later, in a 1793 letter to Jeremy Belknap, Little wrote that "In my several perigrinations [sic], chiefly for innocent [sic] amusement, I made many observations upon the natural Advantages of the Country and the progressive Stages of Vegetaation, with their periods of Maturity, particularly of the garden and field Vegetables, of which I made minutes, from the Town [of] Wells, on my way, to indian Old Town on Penobscot river": Daniel Little to Jeremy Belknap, 4/5/1793, Belknap Papers, MHS.

northeastern frontier of the new United States, the conflict raged between reason and order and emotion and fear, the former Old Lights arguing increasingly for a perspective of a loving God of hope and salvation, the latter New Lights retaining the older Calvinistic argument of a God of vengeance and damnation. "Too many by some unhappy mistakes have concluded that Christ came to destroy men's Lives rather than to save them & in their Convictions of Sin, sink in despair, not attending to his Character as a Savior most compassionate & powerful." Too many of the people of the eastern frontier had "occasion" to hear a message consisting of "frightful Images" of certain Damnation w[hic]h some noisy Zealots under ye name of Ministers have made the chief Subject of their Declamations." Little had quite the opposite view, and pitied such people. "I feel myself attached to no party or persuasion. I wave all Controversies about Modes & Mysteries, & mean to preach a Gospel of Peace and holiness." As a result, "I have ye Pleasure of Seeing a Number who appear to be ye meek & joyful followers of Christ." But the toil was often great for the sixty-one year old Little. "My various removes & multiplicity of Cares & duties have sometimes been a little fatiguing but ye hope that this last Labor of my Ministry may be accepted & blessed of ye Lord is a constant refreshment & support." Many people had responded to Little's message, and wanted more. "Several Towns earnestly desire your Association," he told Stevens, "or their other Neighbours to look out [for] some wise & pious Ministers to settle among them. Their disposition & ability is such as would give a pious Candidate a pleasing Prospect of Comfort &

Usefulness."[96]

To Jeremy Belknap, a longtime friend to whom Little had grown closer because of the journey to Mount Washington during the previous year, Little wrote a more descriptive letter of the religious sentiments brought about by his journey to the east. He informed Belknap on August 10th that he had "visited most of the Settlements on Penobscot River and as far Eastward as Frenchman's Bay." He felt that his efforts, a pastor traveling among distant people solely for their own benefit, "has rendered me more happy in removing the Prejudices of Some against a regular Clergy, which a Number of lay enthusiastic Teachers had propagated, and convincing others of the Importance of a speedy Settlement of the Gospel among them." His ministrations to individuals had brought "Tears of Repentance" and "Tears of Joy." Many of these people had heard a "gloomy," adversarial message from people bringing a message of doom. Little, on the contrary, preached a "joyful Sacred" message of "Good Tidings to all People." As a result, "I never had so full evidence of the certain and blessed Effects of the Gospel as the Gospel of Peace and Grace." Notwithstanding the "Difficulties and hardships" of the journey, Little felt real "contentment and Joy" in his actions. Thinking and preaching about the goodness of God was reflected in his own demeanor and feelings. He felt so good that, he told his friend, "I Wish to fill up the little Time before me in works of Goodness, with growing Diligence and Delight."[97]

---

96 Little to Stevens, 8/15/1785.

97 Daniel Little to Jeremy Belknap, August 10, 1785, Belknap Papers, MHS.

In a letter to Boston merchant Isaac Smith written after his return to Kennebunk, Little informed Smith, who had donated religious books and bibles to be distributed to those in need, that at Deer Isle, these books had been very welcome. Little had established the congregation at Deer Isle twelve years earlier. Some families had not had "Bibles and religious Tracts" since "their Loss of the same by Fire, during the late War." Here and elsewhere on his 1785 journey Little was able to combat prejudice against religion and empathize with people who were in distress. He believed that many of the distressing experiences of his past, "Incidents beyond human foresight," had given him "easy access to Persons of various opinions and Manners."[98]

Little wrote Smith that the limitations of his journey did not allow him to spend the amount of time he wished among both the English and the Indians to ascertain "Whether a Missionary for the latter or both might not be a Useful Appointment." He wondered, however, "Whether one Attempt should not be made to instruct the only Tribe that now remains in this Commonwealth on the eastern Shoar [sic] into the Duties and Pleasures of the Christian Religion, free from those Pains and Fears that Superstition and Mystery has introduced" by means of Roman Catholicism. Anticipating the goals of his 1786 missionary journey, Little suggested that "Perhaps a Number of their Children might be pleased with being Schollers with the english Children, in a well directed School, at a Small but very agreeable english Settlement within 6 miles of the Indian Old Town. Such an

---

98 Daniel Little to Isaac Smith, September, 1785, Smith-Carter Family Papers, MHS.

Attempt would be no great Expence. It would not be lost as the english Children would certainly reap an Advantage." Little confessed that these "Queries" flowed "from a Desire of humane Happiness without partiallity to any People or Nation." In a postscript, Little informed Smith that "the Indians have a Missionary of their own who resides upon an Island in Penobscot Bay between Deer Island and the Main, well situated for their Fishing and Fowling." Here, at White Island, there were temporary habitations for visiting Penobscots who wished to see the priest and replenish their store of food. Contrary to the aims of the Massachusetts government, Little believed it would be "heighly [sic] beneficial for their Support and Comfort that they become the undisturbed Proprietors of that or a Similar Island in that Neighbourhood of which there are many." Little not only visited Old Town, but White Island as well, where he hoped to speak with the priest, who was "from Home." Little was informed," by whom he did not say, "that their Faith in the Authority of his Office and the Fidelity and Efficacy of his Opperations [sic] is far from being general or pleasingly Established."[99]

Having departed Deer Isle, Little left the eastern part of the bay for the western, and ascended the Penobscot to Castine. "Aug. 24. At Majabegaceduce Barely [sic] Sowed 15 June reaped this Day." He was on his way again soon: "The first week in Sep[tembe]r on my Return Home," he wrote, observing the landscape as he went from Camden to Rockport to the headwaters of the St. Georges River to "Broad bay," or Muscongus Bay, along the Muscongus or

---

99 Ibid.

Medomak River. Here Little "gathered 2 ripe ears of Indian Corn," doubtless with the knowledge of the owner, "on gravelly soil richly folded." By the time he came to the Sheepscot River, "up 30 miles from the Sea," he learned from local inhabitants that "every Vegetable that requires a greater degree of Heat than English Grass and Grain are this year, till past Midsummer, one Week later in the Season, than Usual."[100]

Upon his arrival home in mid-September, Little reflected on what he had learned about religion, agriculture, and the people of the eastern frontier. His inclination toward a Gospel of peace, love, and a forgiving, embracing God was reinforced on this journey. Perhaps the years of war had increased his benevolent attitude toward a God who could scarcely condemn any of His children to everlasting torment. Observing agriculture, he concluded: "It is very obvious that neither the Soil nor the Climate are so favorable to the Growth of Indian Corn as at the Westerly Parts of the Commonwealth yet it is not an unprofitable Article of Husbandry in this Part of the Country, as has been Supposed. I have been well informed that 40 Bushels has been raised by a Western Farmer per Acre on Penobscot River. They have not the Advantage of so long a Summers Heat, nor so intense at any Time, as at the Westward. But the Vegetation here is rapid, for it has less intermission from the Chilliness of the Night Air, than at the Westward. The Soil in the County of Lincoln is excellent for grain and a great part of it very fine for Wheat Barley and Flax and if but 2-thirds of the Peoples labour was devoted to Husbandry instead of Lumber

---

[100] "Minutes of the Progressive Growth and Maturity."

they would Soon have a sufficiency of Bread for their Use and Beef and butter for Market." Little's pastoral ideal did not well accommodate the lumber and shipbuilding industries. Of the Indians, his views had taken a marked change from the time before the war. The horror of war, the fear of destruction and disorder, the willingness of the Penobscot people to stay with the Americans, gave Little pause. "The Children of this Tribe numerous," he reflected—"they appear very easy and contented--no signs of Envy, very grateful and sometimes a little gay." Often it is the children who tell us about ourselves, who reveal the inner workings of a society and culture. And these children were much more than savages: they actually had the qualities that Little hoped his own children would have.[101]

---

[101] Ibid.

6 MISSIONARY TO THE PENOBSCOTS

Rev. Daniel Little's journeys and observations came at the end of scores of years of conflict during which the English settlers who found themselves on the Penobscot River were often disillusioned captives brought to Penobscot Bay and River not by choice. His journeys of 1772 and 1774 did little to dispel the notion that the Penobscots were, like American Indians in general, drunken savages. Little's journeys of 1785 and 1786, however, came at the conclusion of a decade of conflict that featured bloodshed on the eastern frontier—and yet the Penobscot Indians had supported the Americans. Daniel Little was a Congregational clergyman who embraced the ideas of human rights and equality and was willing to extend these rights to others, including Indian Roman Catholics. It would not have been unusual for clergymen of Little's time to have objectified Indians as simply an object of study. But this pious scientist embraced Indians as co-observers of the natural environment, willing to share their respective astonishment in nature and its works—such as the highest mountain, Tadden. Indian children seemed as able to be taught as the children of white settlers. The message is more important than the person, and the message was to teach acceptance of a Christian lifestyle and worldview. Protestant conversion, in Little's mind, was a religious change involving a thoughtful approach toward nature as well as God.

The occasion for Daniel Little's 1786 journey to the Penobscot was an invitation to engage in the task, with his expenses paid, by Richard Cary of Charlestown,

Massachusetts. Cary was a merchant and executor of the estate of Colonel John Alford, a wealthy Charlestown merchant, who bequeathed part of his estate "to charitable uses, private or more public, such as may be thought most agreeable to the mind and will of God." Cary believed that the activities of what would become the Society for Propagating the Gospel were consistent with Alford's directive. Cary knew of Little and his activities among the Penobscot, and decided that Alford's money was "designed principally for the Instruction of the Indians." He therefore, Little recalled in a letter two years later, "engaged me to make a Visit to the Indians there to try their lust for religious instruction and their disposition to have their Children taught the language and Manners of the English." Massachusetts governor James Bowdoin likewise supported Little's "noble design," writing to the town of Kennebunk on July 3rd, 1786: "The Revered Daniel Little, minister of the Gospel at Wells, in this Commonwealth, being employed by a charitable person to go on a Mission to the Tribe of Indians at Penobscot River and its environs, to instruct the said Indians in the knowledge of the Christian Religion, and their children in useful human Literature; I do by these presents request the aid and assistance of the Inhabitants of this Commonwealth to the said Revd. Daniel Little in carrying out so good a design: and I do earnestly recommend it to the Indians who are the objects of his mission, to attend to the Religious instructions of Mr. Little, and to treat him with the respect and regard which his sacred character, and the benevolent design of his going among them deserves."[102]

Rev. Little set forth the day after the Sabbath on July 31st for his new adventure to the eastern settlements and Penobscot people. He spent the night at a tavern in what is today Scarborough. August 1st, he proceeded to Falmouth, where he lunched with his friend Rev. Samuel Deane.[103] That afternoon, he rode to the Rev. Tristram Gilman's home at North Yarmouth, where he spent the night. An August rain prevented his journeying the 2nd, so he stayed at Rev. Gilman's and dined with Dr. Ammi Mitchell and wife. The next day was a fine day for traveling, and he set forth alone from North Yarmouth, but after some refreshment at Hobb's Tavern on the road, he joined a Mr. Hunt, who knew the way and acted as "pilot." They passed through what was called Flying Point (Freeport), then Brunswick, before reaching the Kennebec River. Two ferry crossings brought Little to the Rev. Josiah Winship's home in Woolwich, where he spent the night. The next day Little rode to Wiscasset, where he lunched with Dr. Thomas Rice, one of the commissioners appointed by the Massachusetts General Court to treat with the Penobscot Indians. From Wiscasset, Little continued on to Damariscotta, where he stayed with Colonel Arthur Noble, the chief proprietor of the place. Noble's son

---

102 *Report of the Select Committee of the Society for Propagating the Gospel among the Indians and Others in North America* (Boston: John Wilson and Son, 1856), 5-6; Little, "General Account of the Rise and Progress of the Eastern Mission"; Records of the First Parish.

103 Little had stayed the night at Rev. Deane's on his return journey in October, 1774. Little's 1786 journal, the typescript for which is at the Brick Store Museum, is titled "Journal of Mr. Little's Tour to Penobscot, 1786." Herein the journal will be designated *Journal, 1786*, with page numbers referring to the typed manuscript.

volunteered to pilot Little east to Broad Bay (Muscongus Bay); they soon were joined by others. Little wrote in his journal: "had Col. Fainsworth's company thro' the woods to Georges," the St. Georges River. He put up at Copeland's tavern and prepared for the Sabbath. The people here at the town of Warren had "no settled minister since Oqueut [John Urquhart] left them" a few years before. They worshipped in an old meetinghouse once occupied by Rev. William McClanethan "on the bank of the river ab[ou]t 2 miles off." Little preached the two sermons during the course of the morning and afternoon. "This meeting house a large shell—a plentiful rain just before service—was scarcely a dry spot in the meeting house." Little dined with one of the leaders of Warren, Major Hatevil Libbey, before he returned to his lodgings.[104]

Little reached the Penobscot region on August 7th, having traveled from Warren to Rockport, where he stayed, as he had in 1774, with William Gregory. That afternoon, Little took boat, captained by one Titcomb, from Glen Cove to Isleboro in Penobscot Bay. Little stayed with "my old friend," Captain Job Pendleton, who lived on the southernmost of the islands that make up Isleboro—today it is called Job Island, then it was called Little Long Island. Pendleton and his family "sure received me kindly."[105] The

---

104 *Journal*, 1786, 5. For information about the various clergymen Little stayed with on this part of his 1786 journey, refer to Greenleaf, *Sketches of the Ecclesiastical History*.

105 Everett H. Pendleton, *Brian Pendleton and His Descendants* (1910), 137; Olivia Boucher and Melissa L. Olson, *Isleboro—An Island in Penobscot Bay*: http://islesboro.mainememory.net/page/1049/display.html

next day, as Little awaited a boat to take him north, he "visited a very afflicted family" on the islands, "a middle aged woman, very sensible and pious, on the border of the grave, the mother of 8 children. My conversation with her seemed to be seasonable to her and the many spectators." That afternoon, three men arrived from "Bagwaduce" with the news that the Penobscots had retreated from the head of tide (Bangor) to Old Town; two men who had been that way "found it picked in," secured from attack, and "the inhabitants were alarmed." August 9th, Little proceeded up the Penobscot to the Bagaduce River, where he stayed with Dr. Oliver Mann, who had been a surgeon during the Revolutionary War.[106] Here, Little received a written report of the consternation involving the Penobscots: "Two Indians by name Ausory Neptune & Pictsouk say that, agreeable to promise to Gen. Washington they come to give information of approaching danger to the inhabitants." The two men reported that "a large body of southern Indians had met at Montreal and there held a Council, and had sent a belt of Wampum and a Hatchet," essentially an invitation to do battle, "to a certain Tribe which was also sent to them 5 days ago at Passadunkee," upriver from Old Town. Although conflict with the British had concluded three years before, there continued to be tension along the borders between the United States and British Canada. The United States, having disbanded its military in 1783, had insufficient forces to guard its borders—hence tensions continued to exist. The warlike Indians in apparent cahoots with the British warned that if the Penobscots "did not join them" they would

---

106 Wheeler, *History of Castine*, 220

"destroy the Inhabitants, they would destroy all their women & children by Indians throughout, and that they had assurance from the Governour of Canada to assist them with warlike stores, and if occasion called they would assist them with 9,000 men from St. John's and 7,000 from Canada." This indeed seemed a credible threat; the Penobscots said that "if this news should prove true, they wished to be supplied with ammunition to defend themselves. And as they had always been friendly to the State settlers, they should continue the same for the protection of the Inhabitants as well as themselves, and that they would give any information they tho't would be beneficial to them." In response, the men of Bagaduce "sent two men up," one of whom was Colonel Lowell, "to the Indians [at Old T]own to enquire further from whom they have not as yet receiv'd any certain intelligence." Meanwhile, Little waited.[107]

For the next three days, Little joined the leading men of Bagaduce for lunch, tea, and conversation. He lodged at Captain Isaac Perkin's. He visited the sick, and encouraged those who had not yet embraced Christ to reconsider. Sabbath, August 13th, Rev. Little preached sermons morning and afternoon at "Mr. Lee's store." Colonel Lowell returned from Old Town with a French Canadian who had traveled in the company of Indians from Quebec to Passadumkeag, fifteen miles above Old Town. The Frenchman reported "that the Canada Indians are all quiet," which was confirmed by one of the said Indians who accompanied him. Further evidence that all was well arrived on August 14th in the person of Penobscot chief Orono and men making up five

---

107 *Journal*, 1786, 6-7

large birch-bark canoes. They arrived from the south, having been at Penobscot Bay "fishing and fowling." Little spoke with the Penobscots, informing them of his mission, as well as the coming of commissioners from Massachusetts who were to treat with the Indians about their title to lands in the Penobscot valley. Their canoes were "loaded with provisions, some pots and kettles full of boiled clams, seal fish out in strips, and smashed clams stuck upon long sticks like candlerods, and smoked fish dryed in the smoke, buckets of wild onions, and baskets of cucumbers, a store sufficient for each of their families a month."[108]

Now mid-August, Daniel Little journeyed with Colonel Lowell and one "Mackintive" toward Kenduskeag. Along the way Little met with Colonel Buck and stayed with Captain Grant at Marsh Bay on the Penobscot near Frankfort. The next morning, August 17th, Little and his companions journeyed further north to the region between the towns of Orrington and Brewer; here Little lunched with Captain Brewer, one the first English inhabitants of the region, while Lowell and Mackintive continued on to Kenduskeag. After Little's repast, Lowell returned to inform the pastor that "an Indian priest from New York" had arrived at Kenduskeag aboard a sloop. Little immediately journeyed north to Kenduskeag and met with the priest. The "Indian priest," as Little referred to him, Juniper Berthiaume (whom Little called *Ruthham*), was a Franciscan missionary who had arrived in America with the naval fleet of Comte D'Estaing in November, 1778. The two men talked about the rumors swirling about that the southern Indians, or Iroquois,

---

108 Ibid., 7-8.

were going to join with Canadian Indians to attack. The rumor, according to Berthiaume, began when the Iroquois had threatened to attack the Odanak tribe at St. Francis in Quebec. And the Indian who had spread the rumor was the same one, named Latonais, who had, during the war in 1780, along with a band of Indians friendly to the British, captured then Captain Jonathan Lowder and brought him to Quebec. Lowder, whom Little had met and journeyed with in 1774, had since been released due to war's end, and had returned to the Penobscot. Little later discovered that Berthiaume's account was largely accurate, that the Iroquois who had supported the British in the late war were still working to disrupt the American hold over western New York and Pennsylvania, and had demanded the support of northern Indians, such as Odanak, or face destruction.[109]

Little and Berthiaume spoke for about an hour. Little thought "he appeared a man possess'd of a good natural understanding, talked English, somewhat broken, but so as I understood him pretty well. His dress was a blue coat with a velvet collar—white, tall and pretty well proportioned—his address truly French, except an Indian shrug and toss with his shoulder when he pronounced an emphatic No." This Frenchman who had lived with the Indians long enough to

---

109 Ibid., 8-10, 15-16; Austin J. Coolidge and John B. Mansfield, *A History and Description of New England, General and Local*, vol. 1 (Boston: Austin Coolidge, 1859), 243; Charles H. Lagerborn, "Tested Loyalties and Sense of Obligation: Two Maine Men and the American Revolution *Journal of the American Revolution* September, 2017: https://allthingsliberty.com/2017/09/tested-loyalties-sense-obligation-two-maine-men-american-revolution/; Colin G. Calloway, *The American Revolution in Indian Country: Crisis and Diversity in Native American Communities* (Cambridge: Cambridge University Press, 1995); *America: A Catholic Review of the Week* 26 (1921-1922): 276.

pick up some of their habits "was well equipped with pocket instruments"--one imagines a watch, telescope, and compass. After speaking with Berthiaume, Little visited Seth Noble, a local preacher who had been in northern Maine during the Revolutionary War and had served with Colonel John Allan along the eastern coast; he moved south during or after the war, arrived at the Penobscot in 1786, and sought to gather a church at Kenduskeag. Little and Noble joined ministerial efforts, sharing preaching duties. For the Sabbath of August 20th, Little preached at "Capt. Brean's barn." The next day he went upriver a few miles "to see if the Indians were come in." They had not, so he joined Noble and others for a meeting of hymn singing. Noble, an active man of indelicate manners, a good speaker and better drinker, had a good voice.[110]

Father Berthiaume stayed temporarily with a Capt. Robert Treat, a Revolutionary War veteran and early inhabitant of the Penobscot valley who lived on the Kenduskeag River; he was well-known to the Penobscots. Berthiaume and Little "dined" together; Berthiaume informed Little that "he was born at Quebeck, his father dying, his mother carried him to France for an education. 8 years ago he came to St. Peter's, Newfoundland, from thence he went to the West Indies, & from thence he came in Count DeEstang's fleet to America, thence to Boston, and from thence by order of [the General] Court as Missionary to the Indians of Penobscot" shortly after the American defeat at Castine in 1779. "He lived at fort Halifax" on the

---

[110] *Journal, 1786*, 10; Bangor *Historical Magazine*, 4(1889): 193-194; Varney, *Gazetteer*, 99; *History of Penobscot County*, 531

Sebasticook River. The General Court dismissed him in 1782 because of rumors that he was disloyal, but re-instated him shortly thereafter, where he took "up residence at White Island in Penobscot Bay." Berthiaume claimed "that he preached at Versailles before he left France," but Little was dubious of the claim, "by his manner of speech." In response to Little's plan to teach English to the Penobscots, Berthiaume was doubtful of its success. "He ridiculed the marriage of two Indians last week by Col Becks," believing (as would a Catholic priest) that such a secular marriage was null. Berthiaume invited Little aboard his sloop, by which he had sailed, with the help of an English lad, into Penobscot Bay.[111]

For the next few days, Little stayed at Captain Brewer's, awaiting the arrival of the Massachusetts commissioners. He was ill for several days with a "blind carbunkle" in the groin. August 26th, the commissioners arrived: General Benjamin Lincoln, former Revolutionary War general and Secretary of War under the United States Confederation government; General Israel Putnam, Revolutionary War hero at the Battle of Bunker Hill; and Dr. Thomas Rice, a physician of Pownalborough, judge, statesman, and legislator. These three men had been given the responsibility by the Massachusetts General Court in March, 1786, for negotiating land claims with the Penobscot Indians. Little met with the commissioners, and journeyed with them to Kenduskeag, where he lodged with Seth Noble. The

---

111 *Journal*, 1786, 10-11. Daniel J. Tortora, *Fort Halifax: Winslow's Historic Outpost* (Charlestown, SC: The History Press, 2014), claims that Berthiaume departed the region in 1784—Little's journal shows that he was still in the Penobscot in 1786.

commissioners sent John Marsh, an early settler of the upper Penobscot who lived on Marsh Island in the river adjacent to Old Town, to inform the Penobscots of the arrival of the commissioners. The next day, the Sabbath, 65 Indians arrived at Kenduskeag in 21 canoes. Little, meanwhile, lodged with Captain Treat near the Indian encampment.[112]

The morning of the conference, Little went with Treat to the commissioner's sloop to await the beginning of the ceremony. The commissioners requested that the Penobscots "parade" in such a way as they desired. The four "Chieftains, Orono, Orsong [Orson], Neptune, Neptonbavett [Neptonbovitt], [were] seated on the ground close together in the front on an elegant green near the river." Orono was close to one-hundred years old at this time, having been born at the end of the previous century; he was (reputedly) mixed-race; one tradition believed him to be the son of Baron de Castine. Orono was a devout Catholic who had the reputation as a peaceful man who engaged in war at the last extreme. He supported the Americans against the British during the Revolutionary War. The remaining Penobscots stayed "promiscuously," in Little's words, behind the chiefs. Captains Treat and Marsh, acting as interpreters, led the commissioners to the parade ground, "and the conference began, in the presence of a number of spectators." General Lincoln first addressed the Penobscot chiefs, congratulating "them upon the happy close of the War, in which they had

---

112 *Journal,* 1786, 11; John E. Godfrey, "The Ancient Penobscot, or Panawanskek," *The Historical Magazine,* 1872: http://cprr.org/Museum/BMLRR/Penobscot.html. The resolution passed by the General Court appointing and instructing the commissioners is reproduced in *Acts and Resolves of the Commonwealth of Massachusetts, 1786-1787* (Boston: Wright & Potter, 1893), 315-317.

been our faithful friends & brethren." He brought "kind intentions" from the government of Massachusetts, aiming "to settle their landed claims to mutual satisfaction." The Indians responded: "We desire to bless God that you are come, and are glad that our hearts are linked with the Americans. We will now answer you to what you demand." The commissioners requested that the Indians inform them of their claims, and retired to allow the chiefs to consider. When the chiefs indicated they were ready, the commissioners returned, and the Indians said: "We claim down to a small stream below Old Town one mile above [William] Colbourn's [in what is today Orono]; if the English come nearer, our dogs will do them damage, and make a quarrel." At this point the chiefs handed the commissioners "a bundle of papers, upon which the Comm[issioners] retired." Upon consultation, the commissioners responded: "We are glad you express so much satisfaction in seeing us here. We wish you to remember you relinquished your right to this part of the country" during the French-Indian War "to Governor Pownal, and that what you now hold is by the doings of the Provincial Congress in the year 1775; which is 6 miles on each side of the River from the head of the tide" at Bangor. "On this you are now to rest your claims. If you hold only 6 miles next the river, when we settle our land back of that, it will destroy your hunting ground, which we shall be unwilling to do. We propose to give you a larger tract up the river, better for hunting and two Islands in the bay." Upon deliberation, the chiefs responded: "We don't think it right to remove any further up the river. We wish to do nothing but what is right." The commissioners responded that they wished the Penobscots to relinquish control of the six miles width of valley from Old Town to Bangor. In return they proposed that the Penobscots could have control over the lands to the north "on all branches of the river above Pasquattaguess [Piscataquis] on the West side, and Montawanskeag [Mattawamkeag] on the East side." After some consideration, the Penobscots responded "that the 6 miles was their land, and if they moved the bound further up, they expected to be paid for it." The Penobscots requested "Blankets, Powder & Shot, and Flints," to which the commissioners agreed: "You shall have 350 Blankets, 200 Pounds of Powder, and shot and Flints in proportion, at the time when you sign the papers for the ratification of the agreement." Four persons, including Daniel Little, witnessed the agreement. "The conference closed at 2 o'clock." The commissioners requested that the Penobscots not "spread groundless reports of hostile intentions," per the recent rumors of aggression, "but carefully inform the Inhabitants of anything necessary to their safety." Everyone "parted with general joy." The commissioners provided food, "and the Indians regaled themselves, & then went in different parties up the river."[113]

Daniel Little's purpose in journeying to the Penobscot was not, of course, the same purpose as the commissioners; Little hoped to reach out to the Penobscots to bring the Protestant understanding of Christianity to them, which required an understanding of English culture, especially the

---

113 *Journal*, 1786, 11; *Commissioners Conference with the Indians at Penobscot in 1786*, Brick Store Museum, Kennebunk, Maine, 52-55; William D. Williamson, "Notice of Orono, Chief at Penobscot," *Collections of the Massachusetts Historical Society*, 3rd series, volume 9 (Boston: Little and Brown, 1846).

English language. Several days after the conference, Little journeyed to Kenduskeag, and while staying with Captain Treat "conversed with 4 Canadian Indians" as well as a Passamaquoddy woman "who understood English." He was doubtless discovering the truth of his friend Jeremy Belknap's words that "this mode of preaching by an interpreter is very tedious and clumsy. It may do once in a while for a stranger; but a missionary ought certainly to understand the language of his hearers." August 31st, Little rented a horse and paid a guide, one Lovejoy, to take him north upriver to William Colbourn's, "the uppermost settlement" where the English resided nearby the Penobscot people. "Unhappily" two incidents plagued his visit: one, "on my way fell off my horse, & so bruised my right side as to be unable to stoop forward without pain"; second, an English trader named Burley "had been selling rum to the Indians as they returned from the Treaty, and rendered them unfit for conversation"--and much else. There were "7 families in this neighbourhood very poor and ignorant. I invited their children to attend the School tomorrow—prepare them for an admission of the Indian Children if they should send them." September 1st, near what is today Orono, at a place that Little called *Rumfeekhungurs*, he opened the school. He invited Penobscot passersby to observe "the mode of reading and writing"; they "seemed to be pleased." One student, Tonnis, "could understand some English, from whom I learnt to pronounce their names for numbers: 1 Pausuck, 2 Neese, 3 Neush, 4 Yough, 5 Nollum or Parrence, 6 Noughnatunk, 7 Tombowen, 8 Sansuck, 9 Holenway, 10 Mats'tak, 11 Hoquatoneous, 12 Nuquittance Causauncou, 20 Neszinkscou. The 10 first I took from an Indian's mouth, the

10 last an Englishman." The next morning Little's school had "11 schollers, all but 5 know but little more than their letters." Little lunched with a Catholic teacher of the Indians, "Moris Bertheamer," who was perhaps related to and worked with Father Berthiaume, discussing the "usefulness of Schools for the Indians, to which he consented, and said he would see all the Indians together tomorrow on the Sabbath, and would propose it to them." Moris Bertheamer had apparently proposed, or wanted to propose, to the Massachusetts General Court for a land grant near Old Town so that "he would reside and minister to the Indians on the while the School and protestant Minister resided & officiated." He attended Little's school in order to learn English more proficiently.[114]

The next day, the Sabbath, Little sent his interpreter, Capt. Marsh, to Old Town to inquire after the Indians and their interest in the school. He found the town mostly deserted, as the tribe had ascended the Penobscot to Mattawamkeag River "to supply themselves with food from their eel pots which they left set and to secure their Corn from the Bears." Marsh returned with Father Berthiaume. Little spent part of the following day, September 4th, with Berthiaume, who agreed to go up to Old Town and return with Orono and some Indian children. Meanwhile, Captain Marsh worked with Little in translating the Lord's Prayer into Penobscot. For well over a century, Protestant

---

114 *Journal*, 1786, 12-13. In a 1781 petition to the General Court, Juniper Berthiaume referred to a "Linguister" who helped him: perhaps this was Moris Bertheamer (Or, Berthiaume? Was he related?): James P. Baxter, ed., *Documentary History of the State of Maine*, vol. 19 (Portland: Lefavor-Tower, Co., 1914), 303; Jeremy Belknap, *Journal of a Tour from Boston to Oneida, June, 1796* (Cambridge, M.A.: John Wilson and Son, 1882), 24.

missionaries to the North American Indians had debated what was the best approach to bringing the *Word* to their charges: to learn the indigenous language so to sermonize, pray, and translate the Bible, or to teach the Indians English so that they could read the Bible for themselves, which was the Protestant way. Little opted to embrace both approaches. Assuming that the Abenakis of Maine would speak a similar language to the southern Algonquians of Massachusetts, Little brought a copy of the Bible translated into the Algonquian tongue by the seventeenth-century missionary John Eliot. But the language was foreign to the Penobscots. Later, Little discovered an Abenaki vocabulary created by Rev. Ammi Cutter of North Yarmouth. The Indians about Saco spoke a similar language to the Indians about Penobscot. Endeavoring, then, to pursue language as a means of conversion, the next morning Little held school for his students, teaching them English, and at the same time worked with Captain Marsh "to perfect my Vocabulary" of Penobscot words. Berthiaume and Orono not arriving the next day, Little departed from Colbourn's for Kenduskeag to prepare for the installment of Seth Noble as minister to the people of what would become Bangor. Little spent several days in rest and study, working on his vocabulary of the Penobscot language. He noted in his journal that this area of the Penobscot was busy with surveyors sent by the Massachusetts government--the lands of the eastern frontier were being surveyed, sold, and settled. The years after the end of the war in 1783 featured energetic attempts by the thirteen states, united loosely under the Confederation, to place as much of the territory heretofore under British and French control under their own jurisdiction. Such was the pressure on the Penobscot (as well as the many other Indian tribes throughout the frontier regions of the thirteen states) to renegotiate their land claims.[115]

The installation of a Congregational minister in eighteenth-century New England involved ceremony, prayer, sermonizing—all of the religious formalities that Congregationalists could muster. Usually up to half a dozen of neighborhood clergymen would arrive for such an installation, one praying, one giving the sermon, one giving the right hand of fellowship. But for Seth Noble's installation, there was only one minister, Rev. Daniel Little. This could have concerned Little, and indeed he could have refused to install Noble until there were other clergy present. Little, however, believed in the beliefs and feelings rather than the forms and rituals of religion, so he was all too willing to install Seth Noble, in the name of New England Congregationalism, by himself. Sabbath day, therefore, September 10, 1786, in an orchard next to the Kenduskeag River, Daniel Little, in the presence of a large congregation, "gave [Seth Noble] his Pastoral charge and the right [hand] of fellowship. The people are satisfied, without offering any objection."[116]

After waiting six days, Little sent Capt. Marsh to Old Town to inquire "what is the reason the Indians do not appear; and invite them down to my lodgings for a Conference." That afternoon, Berthiaume arrived from

---

115 *Journal,* 1786, 13-14; Bourne, *History of Wells and Kennebunk,* 712; *Collections and Proceedings of the Maine Historical Society,* 2nd Series, Vol. 4 (Portland: Maine Historical Society, 1893), 416.

116 *Journal,* 1786, 14-15.

upriver with the news that the Penobscots had met and decided against the English school, as "they were jealous that their children would be taught a different Religion." The next day, September 13th, Capt. Marsh arrived with corroborating information. "All hopes of any further information being at an end," Little, extremely disillusioned, walked six miles downstream to Capt. Treat's; along the way Berthiaume joined him, and they "conversed . . . in Latin—found he could speak pretty well." But Daniel Little was exhausted. Even so, ever the pastor, once he reached his lodgings, he "visited an old widow, in great affliction in body and mind." Little slowly made his way downriver, lodging with familiar people, such as Captain Brewer. He hired two men to guide him downriver to Marsh Bay, where he stayed once again with Captain Grant--"a kind, hospitable family. Enjoyed the Sabbath at Marsh Bay, or Frankfort, then set forth for Sandy Point, where he supped, then walked to Fort Point, where he stayed with Robert Treat's older brother, Joshua Treat. Here Little briefly conversed with "two ancient Indians" who spoke of the past under the French along the Penobscot River and Bay. The next day, Little wrote, he "spent the forenoon with those Juleps in learning the Indian language."[117]

Henceforth, journeying home, Little traveled to Bagaduce, where he stayed with a Mr. Black and converted Mr. Lee and his family to Christianity. Dr. Mann

---

117 Ibid., 15-16. By *julep*, Little seemed to be implying that the "ancient Indians" he conversed with were mildly intoxicated yet pleasant, for at this time a julep "is commonly understood" as "an agreeable liquor, designed as a vehicle for medicines of greater efficacy, or to be drank after them, or to be taken occasionally as an auxiliary." W. Lewis, *The New Dispensatory* (London: Nourse, 1781), 609.

accompanied Little on his journey across the bay, though bad weather made them halt at Isleboro. He took Capt. Little's sloop across the bay toward Camden, but a southerly made them put in at Ducktrap, west of Isleboro and south of Belfast. Little stayed with General George Ulmer, and on the Sabbath, September 24th, preached for the inhabitants of Ducktrap. The following morning he traveled by foot south. "Had a meeting on the road for the baptizing of a number of children. Travelled 6 miles on the side of the bay to Megunteehook" on the road to Camden. Here Little found his horse, whom he had boarded with a Mr. Creepner, well. He set off west to return home, feeling very tired. Stayed with Colonel Farnworth at Muscongus Bay. Along the way stopped at Thomas Rice's, who rode with Little for a distance, no doubt talking about the conference with the Penobscots. By the time Little arrived at Kennebunk he was "not a little fatigued."[118]

Little's fatigue was of the body and the spirit. The many visits, the years of study, the work to know the Penobscot language, the labor creating a vocabulary, had come to naught. The unwillingness of the Penobscots to work with him to learn English, to consider the Protestant way of life, added to the burden of travel, spending hours on foot and on horseback, staying at hostels with varying degrees of comfort. Little was sixty-two years old, and this journey of two months wore on him. He was clearly aware, however, that he had gifts that made him a successful messenger for God. He was impatient with the standard teachings of the New England clergy, and was willing to expunge from his

---

118 *Journal*, 1786, 16-17.

mind and teaching such terms as "trinity, atonement, election, native depravity."[119] Like other clergy who had experienced the devastating effects of the American Revolution—the violence, bloodshed, and evil of war—Little relaxed his beliefs in the Calvinist theology upon which he had been raised. He focused more of his attention on a singular Creator, a Deity of Love who created all humans and, Little reasoned, did not betray such love with damnation.

Daniel Little was a person of an open mind willing to see the varied colors and hues that make up humanity. He had a singular gift for empathy, which he revealed time and again on his journeys. Edward Bourne summed up his character thus: "Mr. Little may well be classed with the eminent men of the last century; not so much on account of any intellectual prominence, as from his unwearied devotion to the great object to which he had dedicated his life."[120]

---

[119] Bourne, *History of Wells and Kennebunk*, 720

120. Ibid., 708.

7 APOSTLE OF THE EAST

At some point late in life, when Daniel Little was no longer engaged in missionary journeys and was, perchance, reflecting on days gone by, he told his friend and fellow minister of the Gospel Timothy Alden a story. Alden recalled the story when in 1801 the Penobscot chief Orono died, aged 113. "Mr. Little," Alden wrote, "was sent on a mission many years since, into the Penobscot country, where he became acquainted with Orono. On a certain time, in a pleasant familiar manner, he asked Orono in what language he prayed. Orono made no reply, but assumed a grave aspect. Mr. Little repeated his question; but Orono, without uttering a single word, looked still more grave. After a little interval, Mr. Little, clapping Orono on his shoulders, said, come, Orono, come, tell me in what language you say your prayers, Indian, French, or Latin? He knew the French to be well understood by the tribe, from their intercourse with the Canadians. Orono, with a solemnity of countenance, which delighted Mr. Little, lifted up his hands and his eyes towards heaven, and said, *no matter, Great Spirit know all languages*."[121]

Perhaps this incident occurred in 1786, when Little opened his Indian school near Old Town, a school that was ultimately short-lived, doubtless in part because of Orono's opinion. Little wrote his sponsor Richard Cary that the influence of Father Berthiaume had a negative impact on Little's Protestant English school. But perhaps more,

---

121 Alden, *Collection of American Epitaphs and Inscriptions*, 10-11.

although "a small part of them were desirous to have their children taught the language and manners of the English, . . . all of them were apprehensive that their religion would be in danger; [they] wished to know why their children could not be taught to read and write by a master of their own religious persuasion." The familiarity, betrayed in Alden's anecdote, that Little reportedly had with the Penobscot Orono, reveals the honesty of conviction and wisdom of understanding of Orono toward religiosity. Ultimately language and denomination matter little in the interaction of individual human with God. Alden's anecdote did not include a retort from Little to Orono, because there could be, after all, nothing more to say.[122]

Little's attempt to teach the Penobscot the Protestant ways of Christianity, to turn them from their Catholic upbringing, was, in retrospect, doomed to failure. He was opposed by a Catholic priest who was just as educated, and better known to the Penobscot, than Daniel Little, a mere visitor. Moreover, Little unfortunately associated himself with the government of Massachusetts; at the same time that he was attempting to convert the Indians to his way of life, he was also trying to convince them that they had no clear title to the land upon which they had resided and hunted for centuries. English Protestants had defeated French Catholics in war, a war that was political as well as religious. Orono had lived through the many wars of empire between the French and English during the eighteenth century. The English and Protestants took control of the Penobscot region

---

[122] *The Society for Propagating the Gospel Among the Indians and Other in North America, 1787-1887* (No POP: University Press, 1887), 29.

in 1759. A government, the colony then the state of Massachusetts, hereafter exercised power, both political and religious power. But for someone as filled with devotion and faith as Orono, one's relationship with God has very little to do with politics and religion.

Little persevered, however. He was called to a mission and he was not going to give up easily. Although, as he wrote Samuel Phillips in 1788, he believed his ministry to the Penobscots were but "feeble attempts to promote that noble design," he still believed in perseverance in a "difficult, tho' not as yet . . . altogether hopeless task." He took hope, no doubt, in the formation of a new society in 1787, modeled upon other similar missionary organizations in America and Great Britain: the Society for Propagating the Gospel Among the Indians and Others in North-America. The members of this new society, located in Boston, "believing that to civilize [the Indian] is one great and necessary steps towards christianizing them," bought materials to teach husbandry, helped to build school houses, and purchased "books upon pious and practical subjects." With limited funds, they focused their attention on tribes living within the new states, hoping in time to branch out further west across the continent. As the Great Commission involves all people, not just the indigenous, the society also wished to reach out to white settlements, particularly on the Eastern Frontier. The Massachusetts General Court chartered and funded, in part, this society, which brought together many of the Protestant leaders of Massachusetts.[123]

---

[123] *Brief Account of the Society for Propagating the Gospel Among the Indians and Others in North-America* (Boston, 1798), 2-4.

One of the sponsors of the new society, the president of the Massachusetts state senate, Samuel Phillips, Jr., in 1787 engaged Daniel Little to journey on behalf of Society for Propagating the Gospel, this time focused on the English settlers of the state of Maine. During his 1787 and subsequent missionary journeys, Abiel Abbot, a young man from Wilton, New Hampshire, in the southwestern portion of the state, joined the venerable Rev. Little. Abbot was a twenty-two year old recent Harvard graduate trained for the ministry and scholarship. He was an early member of the Society for Propagating the Gospel. Little apparently kept a journal of this 1787 trip that has not survived, except for a small snippet. Abbot composed a narrative account short on details and long on religious platitudes. And the Kennebunk parish provided a 125-word description.[124]

We learn, for example, that the two men departed June 13th, and traveled northeast following, we might guess, along the coast until they reached the Kennebec River, which they took north to Hallowell (near present Augusta). They sought a copy of a local "Census" to provide them with, according to Abbot, "the best information of the general state of the country, and particularly of the more infant town and plantations, that we might better arrange and proportion our services to answer the general design of the mission." From Hallowell, they proceeded northwest through Readfield to Sandy River (Farmington), and another dozen or so miles northwest "to the uppermost settlement on s[ai]d river."

---

[124] Little, "General Account of the Rise and Progress of the Eastern Mission"; "Account of the Tour & Mission of the Rev. Mr. Little in Company with the Rev. Abiel Abbot, in the y ear 1787," Brick Store Museum; "Extracts from the Rev. Daniel Little's Journal of 1787," Brick Store Museum; *Records of the First Parish*.

Along the way they provided "20 sermons" for the locals. They returned back to Hallowell, rested, then journeyed up the Kennebec River, through modern Augusta, to the old Indian town of Norridgewock. More than sixty years ago, during Dummer's War, the Abenaki Indian village had been attacked and sacked by English militia in reprisal for attacks on New England towns. The Catholic priest Father Sebastian Rale had been killed. From here, Little and Abbot journeyed thirty miles further upriver "to the uppermost plantation, called Caratunk," where the Caratunk Falls are near the present town of Solon. The two ministers "officiated in all the towns on said river above fort Western," Augusta. Whereupon, Little and Abbot returned back down the Kennebec, rested two days at Hallowell, then set out on a journey to the Penobscot region, "called the Waldo patent, and up the bay of Penobscot as far as Belfast," which Little had visited thirteen years before. Along the way Little observed to Abbott that "his first services among the people" of a place "were more arduous, and less successful, than after he was pretty well known to them, and they to him." They crossed the bay from Belfast to Castine, journeyed up the Bagaduce River to what Abbot called Penobscot, the ancient Pentagoet, plantation Number 3 settled by David Marsh. Here they crossed over to visit Little's old friends at Blue Hill, then returned to Bagaduce. Ascending the Penobscot River to the Kenduskeag, they stopped along the way at Bucksport to celebrate the Sabbath with the inhabitants. At Kenduskeag, Little and Abbot lodged with Little's friend

John Brewer.[125]

Here, on September 18th, Little asked Brewer "to give me a particular account of the death of an Indian last spring which was reported to be a murder by some of the Inhabitants." Andrew Gilman, who frequently hunted with the Penobscot Indians along the upper reaches of the Penobscot River, had joined a hunt with an Indian named Peal, his wife, and sixteen-year old stepson. During the course of the hunt they acquired many furs, which they deposited at Peal's camp. But they could not agree on the division: Peal wanted a third, and his wife and stepson wanted a third; Gilman thought it should be a 50-50 split. They took a few furs to trade for rum at Captain Robert Treat's at Kenduskeag, and became intoxicated. A few days later, Gilman returned to Peal's camp with a young man named James Page. Gilman and Page ran into Archibald McPhetres and another Indian named Sabbatus, who journeyed to Treat's for more rum, returning to Peal's camp. All became intoxicated, and disputes arose about the division of the furs. The argument led to violence, in which Page killed Peal; Page claimed it was self-defense. Page, Gilman, and McPheters departed, leaving the dead body (Peal's wife and son had escaped the violence). The next morning, Sabbatus awakened from his drunken stupor, found Peal's body and came upon his widow; Sabbatus took the widow in his canoe to Old Town. Meanwhile, Peal's stepson soon arrived seeking revenge. But the sachems, such as Orono, told the young man and his comrades: "We are

---

[125] "Account of the Tour & Mission of the Rev. Mr. Little in Company with the Rev. Abiel Abbot," 20; *Records of the First Parish*; Varney, *Gazetteer*, 432.

under Massachusetts government. See what Gen. Court do first, then we know what to do." They sent word to Captain Brewer, who "apprehends Gilman, Page & Mr. Fetters [McPheters], & carries them the next day before Justice [Simeon] Fowler." The justice examined the body of Peal, and determined that it was the wound of a musket ball, so ordered Brewer, the sheriff, to take the three men to gaol in Pownalborough to await trial. However, "the Indians not being acquainted with the laws of the commonwealth, did not appear at the Supreme Court to support their complaint"; the three accused were therefore released.[126]

From the Penobscot region, the two missionaries "went on our retrograde tour, officiated transiently at sundry places till we arrived to the new plantations on Amoriscoggin [Androscoggin] river, in the county of Cumberland." At some unknown location along the Androscoggin, Little and Abbot obtained "the best information of the number and extent of the settlements on that river and its vicinity." The season was advanced into mid-autumn, so they eschewed journeying into central Maine, and contented themselves with traveling to York County, the region of the Saco, Kennebunk, and Piscataqua rivers. Little returned home for a week to rest while Abbot continued the missionary work. They reunited in early October at Sanford on the Mousam River. Rev. Little officiated at the ordination of Moses Sweat to the south parish of Sanford. Thereupon, during the month of October, the two missionaries journeyed north of Sanford

---

[126] "Extracts from the Rev. Daniel Little's Journal of 1787, 56-57; "Account of the Tour & Mission of the Rev. Mr. Little in Company with the Rev. Ahiel Abbot," 16; *History of Penobscot County* (Cleveland: Williams, Chase & Co., 1882), 533; *Bangor Historical Magazine* 2(1896-1897): 242.

toward the Ossipee River valley, visiting "all the new towns and plantations" on this river and on the upper Saco. Winter coming so as "to render it inconvenient for the people to attend our services, and hazzardous [sic] to our health, we judged that the remaining part of the services," such as communion, baptism, and prayer, "would be more beneficial to the people if given them at a milder season." Over the course of their extensive four-and-a half-month tour, the two missionaries met with people individually or in small groups, so that "personal prejudices have been removed, errors corrected, and lessons of family religion handed home to the bosoms of parents and children." In addition, Little and Abbot convinced many of the leaders of these small, burgeoning frontier communities of the necessity and benefits of organizing and supporting a congregational church. The missionaries promised to contact the Society for Propagating the Gospel to send the names of the potential candidates for their local congregations.[127]

Little spent the winter contemplating his missionary work, and the efficacy of energetic workers on behalf of Christ going among the ignorant, often illiterate, people of the Maine frontier, combating the enthusiastic, erroneous (if well-intentioned) message of self-appointed messengers not sanctioned by established missionary establishments as the Society for Propagating the Gospel. By May, 1788, the agreement with the Penobscots of two years previously having not yet been fulfilled, Governor John Hancock asked Daniel Little if he would join the role of government

---

[127] "Account of the Tour & Mission of the Rev. Mr. Little in Company with the Rev. Abiel Abbot," 18-21.

commissioner to that of missionary. Little initially was reluctant to put his family and parish through the difficulties of another journey. He wrote Hancock that although "I do not wish to excuse myself from any service to the public compatible with my ability and consistent with my home connections," "as I have been absent from my people a part of the three preceding summers I found it expedient to take their opinion, who have this day concurred with my acceptance of your Excellency's appointment, on condition of my supplying the pulpit without their care or expense." Besides, "I feel very unequal to a business which requires so much patience, delicacy and fortitude," and "nothing but a sense of duty . . . and a condition of some advantages arising from my personal acquaintance with the Indians has induced me to accept [the] appointment." Accordingly, Little rode to Boston at the end of May to meet with Governor Hancock. He departed Boston on June 3rd, rode to Portsmouth then Wells, where he stayed for a day making preparations. He set off for Penobscot on June 7th.[128]

As before, save his 1774 journey, Little took the land route, traveling northeast by horseback, crossing rivers, staying at taverns. It took him nine days to reach Castine on the Bagaduce River, arriving in a canoe fixed with two masts at sunset on the 14th. The agreed upon blankets, powder, shot, and flints for the Penobscots were already being stored at John Lee's store on the Bagaduce River. Little requested Lee to contrive a vessel to take the material upstream to

---

[128] Little, "General Account of the Rise and Progress of the Eastern Mission"; *Bangor Historical Magazine*, 5(1889-1890), 59; "Mr. Little's Tour to Penobscot by Direction of the Governor & Council from June 3 to July 15, 1788" (hereafter referred to as *Journal, 1788*), Brick Store Museum.

Kenduskeag. This Lee did, while Little spent a few days visiting the people of the Bagaduce River, including preaching on the Sabbath, as "they had no minister among them." Thereupon, he "engaged Capt. Brewster [Brewer] & son who lives up the river to assist Capt. Holbrook in removing the articles for the Indians [from] Lees store on board the vessel, and sail up the river with us." Arriving at Kenduskeag in the afternoon, Little proceeded to Captain Robert Treat's, "the interpreter, and gave him written directions to go up the river and inform me as soon as possible whether the Indians were at home and invite them at a public conference at Canduskeag." Little provided Treat with a formal letter on behalf of the Massachusetts government, requesting in detail that he locate the Penobscots at or near Old Town, and bring especially the chiefs back down the river to receive their supplies from the government whereupon they are to "sign the papers for the confirmation of the agreement."[129]

Treat set off upriver accompanied by William Colbourn. He returned the next day with a verbal message from the chiefs of the Penobscot tribe, who informed them that they wished to meet with Rev. Little but did not wish to descend the river to Kenduskeag because on other occasions "their young men were apt to drink," which they wished to forestall by having the commissioner journey to Old Town, where "everything might be done calmly and cooly with us." Little, who wanted his actions to "be consistent with the honour of Govt.," to his credit made the wisest decision not to insist on the Indians coming to meet him, rather that "I would meet

---

[129] *Journal, 1788*, 61-62.

the tribe in their own town (which lies on an island in the river, 12 miles above the head of tide [Bangor,] 14 from Canduskeag) on Saturday." Little was able to gather around him several men of ability and knowledge to help in this endeavor to meet and negotiate with the Indians. Joining Little were Colonel Jonathan Louder, a veteran of military affairs in the Penobscot valley and sometime truckmaster for the Indians; Captain Brewer, Little's good friend by now; Seth Noble, the new clergyman serving these people; Simeon Fowler, the local justice of the peace; John Lee, "who had had the charge of articles for the Indians, and who had used various means to bring forward and complete the treaty"; William Colbourn, who probably knew the Indians better than any of them, except for perhaps Robert Treat, who also accompanied Little. Little asked these men to keep a record of the proceedings, to which he added his own journal.[130]

On Saturday, June 21st, they passed the confluence of the Stillwater and Penobscot rivers, crossing to a large island, "about 7 miles long," situated between the rivers. The men "walked upon said Island in a trackless wood, about 5 miles, when Indian Old Town Island, about 200 acres, open[ed] to view with a thicket of houses on Lower point of said Island, above great Falls." The Penobscot River surrounded the small island. The Penobscots, having awaited their visitors two days, spied them across the river and quickly "a number of their canoes were man'ed with sprightly young men, in which they came over . . . to transport us into town. As we

---

[130] Ibid., 63; Subscriber's Account of Daniel's Little's Meeting with Penobscot Indians, June, 1788, 57-60, Brick Store Museum.

landed, their shore was lined with women and children." The visitors approached the "parade" awaiting them, walking upon a "smooth" path, "about 5 rods in width, lined on each side with a range of houses, built with poles about 6 inches diameter, and the same as under, placed perpendicularly, and covered very neatly with barks in a shingle form." The men were welcomed into the central house by a Penobscot sachem, "who made us very welcome, directing us to take possession of one half the room 20 by 40 which was carpeted with fur." Other sachems now arrived to take their place, along with other men who "place themselves in rank next the Sachems," as well as an elderly sachem, "introduced in memory of past services." The Penobscot set off a cannon nearby to commemorate the beginning of the discussions.[131]

As Rev. Little readied himself to read prepared remarks to the Penobscots, he looked about the room. Only men were present, about fifty of them of varying ages. Little informed the Penobscots of his commission by the government of Massachusetts to settle the agreement made by the commissioners led by General Lincoln in August, 1786. The Massachusetts government had delivered the blankets and other supplies to Kenduskeag for the Indians to retrieve. Little also had with him an agreement for the sachems to "make their mark against the seals, . . . upon their doing this I should give them the parchment in my hand containing the gift of land to them, together with the 300 blankets." The sachems, especially the four leaders Orson Neptune, Orono, Orson (or Orsong), and Neptune Bowot, in response withdrew for a half hour to consult, then returned. Their

---

[131] *Journal, 1788*, 63-64.

spokesperson, Orson Neptune, said:

> We are thankful to see Mr. Little here and desire to be remembered to the Governor and Council, and are glad to see all well here together. The king of France says we are all one, and it is all peace, and the king of England says it is peace, though it was war sometime ago. Brother, we are all one, we don't talk of hurting another. We live here to serve God. We all live together. We and our children mean to help each other. We don't mean to take any lands from you. If Anybody takes away our land from us, it must be king George[,] for Gen. Court and General Washington promised us we should enjoy this country. General Washington and General Court Told us if anybody was going to take our lands from us, they would let us know it. They told us if they knew anything was doing against us, they would tell us. Brother, now we are all here together, when we were at Canduskeag we had not a right understanding of matters, and all the young men were not all collected, and we were pressed to make that Treaty contrary to our inclinations. Brother[,] God put us here. It was not king of France or king George. We mean to stay on this Island. The great God put us here, and we have been on this island 500 years, and we have been of the French king religion, and mean to be so always. From this land we make our living. This is the general speech of all our young men. We don't know anything about writing. All that we know we mean to have a right heart and a right tongue. Brother, we don't incline to do anything about the Treaty made at Canduskeag, or that writing (pointing to the paper I held open to them with a fine explanation of it.)[132]

At this point, Orson turned to Little's interpreter, Captain Treat, and asked: "Is not Mr. Little a Minister?" Hearing the

---

[132] Ibid., 64-65, 67.

affirmative, he said to Little: "Brother Ministers ought not have anything to do in public business about land. Today is Saturday, they ought to be preparing for the Sabbath. There are other gentlemen who might act in this business." Unaffected, Little responded:

> Fathers & Brothers, of the Penobscot Tribe. It is true the Great God placed you here to serve him; and it is true that the king of France and the king of England and we, all one all at peace now. But you must remember that the lands you now hold is by the doings of Massachusetts Government. At Canduskeag Gen. Lincoln told you in Gov. Pownals day, in a former war against us, you lost all your lands in this part of the country. That in the year 75 Massachusetts Govt. gave you 6 miles on each side of the river from the head of tide, on which you must rest your claims, to which you then consented; and you must remember Gen. Lincoln called witnesses to what was then said and done—Col. Edy, Capt. Colburn, Mr. Noble and myself. Here are three of those witnesses present (the witnesses were called forward and presented—the Indians were silent.) For those two strips of land by the river, Massachusetts Govt. according to the agreement, made by Gen. Lincoln, now gives you up in the country 4 times as much land for hunting, two Islands in the Bay, with all the town and Islands in the river you now occupy, with 350 Blankets. You shall be assured of the enjoyment of the religion of the king of France without interruption as long as you please. I am not here today as a minister, but a Commissioner. I saw the Gov[r]. and Council less than 20 days ago; what they then spoke I now have a right to speak. You are sensible, Govt. has fulfilled all on their part of the Treaty made at Canduskeag. You say your young men [weren't] present then. Your fathers used to ask for the children. The same Fathers and Sachems, that were there, are now here. Will you make your marks for your names against these seals on this paper

which tells what land you give to Govt., and accept of this parchment, which is the act of General Court giving land to you, and then receive the blankets, will you do this or not?[133]

At the noon hour, the Penobscot men, who had been silent except for the speaker Orson, paused for prayer with the ringing of a bell. They prayed for ten minutes, appealing "to Heaven, as given them a secure right to the soil all the Sachems rose up from the ground on which they sat and stood in a posture for a minute expressive of an appeal to the great God of the truth of their declarations." Thereupon the sachems responded: "We don't know anything about writing. We have put our hands to many papers at Albany, New York and elsewhere; but we will not put our hands to that paper now, nor any more papers now, nor any other time forever hereafter." They added: "All that we know . . . is that we mean to have a right heart and a right tongue." Little responded: "Although you refuse to put your hands to the agreement made at Canduskeag by words and witnesses, yet you m ay expect Govt. will abide by it, and expect the same from you. If you break such solemn agreements, you must not expect prosperity from heaven, or any future favours from Govt., but if you fulfill treaties faithfully in time of any future want or distress, you might expect Govt. would be kind to you and help you." During the whole, "not a word spoken, or smile expressed by any of them, except their moderator or Orator, and a few directing words by the Council to assist their speaker."[134]

Having been stonewalled in this endeavor, Little now

---

[133] Ibid., 65-66.

[134] Ibid., 66-67.

turned to the issue of the death of the Indian Peal in 1787. He told the sachems that the state of Massachusetts would pay to send two sachems and relevant witnesses to the crime to Pownalborough to attend a court proceeding, accompanied by Colonel Brewer. The Penobscots expressed their confidence that the court would do justice, and asked for several days to consider the matter. The conference concluded, Little and his escort departed; young men brought them across the river from Old Town. Treat and Colbourn led them back to the confluence with Stillwater River, which they crossed, then canoed two miles south to Kanduskeag. On the 22nd, the Sabbath, Little preached one sermon, Rev. Noble the other. Orono arrived from Old Town to tell Little that the tribe would send no one to Pownalborough to observe court proceedings respecting Teal's death. "Peal's wife and son were at Pas[s]amaquoddy," the tribe was focused on a summer hunt, and they believed that the court would make a satisfactory conclusion. Little asked Orono of the concern that some tribal members, such as Orson, had about Father Berthiaume. Orono said Berthiaume had "little faults like your priests and all priests." Little then journeyed to Colonel Brewer's, accompanied by Orono and wife. Meanwhile he put into Brewer's care for storage all of the items that were to go to the Penobscots should they sign the treaty. Little spent the next few days in visits and letter-writing, before departing down the Penobscot on Friday for Colonel Buck's house. He took a "Connecticut schooner" from Kenduskeag to what is today Bucksport. Here, as he had done on previous years, Little preached before "a large and serious assembly" who had not enjoyed such an occasion since Little had visited the previous year. Such work was particularly meaningful for Little, still reeling from his failure to establish an Indian school in 1786 and now his failure to achieve the final treaty with the Penobscots for which he had been commissioned. Also gratifying was the impact of his work, as well as the obvious "finger of God," in the change in the demeanor of Major Jonathan Buck, who had gone from a life of drunkenness and profanity to one of sobriety and decorum. "The general testimony of his neighbours says his daily life is uniform, honest, benevolent and devout." From Buck's, Little journeyed east to the settlement of Penobscot on the upper Bagaduce River, where he visited the afflicted and "baptized 7 children." He awaited possible word from the Penobscot tribe that they were agreeable to the treaty—to no avail. On a rainy Sabbath, July 6th, Little led services and preached at Penobscot before "a large assembly" of "attentive people"; he "baptized 5 children." The inhabitants experienced what many other large settlements with scattered populations in early America experienced—division as to where to locate the Meetinghouse. "I wish them a better temper," Little wrote. "If all their zeal was about pure religion, it would not be difficult to find a convenient mountain or vale."[135]

It was time for Little to depart the Penobscot if he wished to attend the court case respecting the murder of Peal at Pownalborough. He joined the ferryman in the evening to cross the upper bay, but "the fog coming in so thick obliged us to go ashore on Long Island [North Isleboro] and lodge." The next day, the fog not abating, they crossed to Duck Trap,

---

[135] Ibid., 66-69.

then hugged the coast south to Camden. Here Little reunited with his horse and set forth south toward Pownalborough. He traveled to Warren, where he had stayed on previous occasions, then the next day journeyed to Pownalborough on the Kennebec River. The courthouse, which still stands, is an imposing three-story structure. Here, Little met (and stayed) with the High Sheriff, Edmund Bridges; he also met with the Grand Jury. Colonel Brewer and Jeremiah Colbourn were present at the proceedings. The case ended in a hung jury. The jurymen requested that Little write a letter to the Penobscots informing them of the result:

> Brothers and Chief Fathers of the Penobscot Tribe. Col. Brewer and Mr. Colburn will tell you that 12 men, good men, met at Kennebec, examined the evidences very carefully about Peal's death, and they could not find light enough to say what punishment was due to the man who killed Peel; whether he killed him in his own defense or with a bad anger they could not tell. If any more light should come between now and next year they will look into the matter again and see that justice be done. Mr. Little sends his love to you all, and sends by Col. Brewer 5 dollars to Peal's widow; and if she should be sick or want support let Col. Brewer and Mr. Colburn know it and she shall be provided for as long as she is a widow.
>
> I am your Father and Brother. Daniel Little[136]

Upon the conclusion of the court proceedings respecting Peal's murder, Little stayed on for three more days, as there was no clergyman to minister to a condemned convict, John McNeal. Little visited the prisoner . . . who appeared very hardened. No signs of contrition of repentance." He was

---

[136] Ibid., 69-70.

apparently a Scot who arrived in Nova Scotia intent on finding one McLary, also a Scot; once he found him, further south in Maine, he killed him. "The trial was solemn." Saturday, as the prisoner awaited his fate, Little "visited and prayed" with him, and also "rode out among the inhabitants" of the Kennebec, visiting "several families." On the Sabbath, June 13th, Little preached at the courthouse, and dined at John Gardiner's a well-known statesman. Before departing for home he returned to the prisoner's cell to pray with the condemned man—"prayed ex tempore." Then he departed for home. Little journeyed south along the Kennebec River to Chops Point, a peninsula jutting into Merrymeeting Bay. He crossed by ferry "at the Chops" (Chops passage, the confluence of the Androscoggin and Kennebec), then continued southwest paralleling the Androscoggin River, then picked up the trail west toward Brunswick, eventually North Yarmouth, where he spent the night. The next day he rode to Portland, then the following day to Kennebunk, where he "found my family and people well."[137]

Looking back on his time spent on the eastern frontier, Little recalled some particularly affecting moments, such as when he "handed one of the testaments to a serious young woman, back in the country, who gave very pleasing marks of pious gladness. She had a religious education before the family removed into the wilderness; tho' poor, yet rich in Scripture, knowledge and gracious experience." He recalled one unnamed community, which he had visited in 1774, where he had left them with religious books, and now, "the happy effects of the pious use of them" continues, though

---

[137] Ibid, 71.

fourteen years had passed.[138]

After a journey of six weeks, Little concluded his journal: "Acknowledge God in all thy ways and he shall direct thy paths. He shall preserve thy going out and thy coming in from this time forth and forevermore. Amen."

---

[138] "A brief Account of the present State of the Society for propagating the Gospel among the Indians and Others in North-America,--with a Sketch of the Manner in which they mean to pursue the Objects of their Institution," MHS. Included in this account was a "Letter from the Rev. Mr. Little, to the Secretary of the Society," November 24, 1790."

8 FINAL JOURNEY

Daniel Little's many journeys on behalf of the Great Commission throughout northern New England earned him the reputation, and eventual official recognition from the government of Massachusetts, as the *Apostle of the East*. There are few records about this honorary title save the anecdotal. One suspects that Little himself would have been a bit embarrassed by such accolades. He was largely a humble man, though his role as a pastor in eighteenth-century New England, especially among people who rarely saw men of the cloth, could have given him sufficient airs that in a less modest person would have led to insufferable haughtiness. Little was always humbled by the task, the mission, and the awe and piety that he felt toward the Creator and His creation.

Besides the troubles, the exhaustion, the separation from family and parish, the dangers, involved in bringing the message to others, there was constant doubt and questioning. Would it in the end matter whether or not the Gospel was brought to people who had lived so long without it, or people who had been converted to a different kind of faith, such as Roman Catholicism? Respecting the Indians, many of Little's contemporaries were unconvinced that these people would embrace Christianity, that their behavior, their way of living, could support a true Christian lifestyle. Even members of missionary organizations, such as the Society for Propagating of the Gospel, were doubtful of the efficacy of the messenger's labors. The same year that Little made his fifth journey to the Penobscot region, at a meeting of the

Society for Propagating the Gospel in Boston, one of its prospective members, a Mr. Dexter, declined joining the organization because "it would be to no purpose to send missionaries among the Indians, while we ourselves set them so bad an example, not acting according to the religion which we profess." Dexter was impatient with the New England Protestantism of his day, and believed that the Calvinist doctrines of sin and atonement, of the elect and reprobate, of providence and predestination, could hardly be embraced by the Indians, particularly those imbued with Roman Catholic doctrines. Dexter, cognizant of the division among Protestants in the late eighteenth century, believed "that, as to the English settlers at the Eastward and elsewhere, they might, if destitute, be supplied with Bibles and other religious books, and read them themselves." What purpose, he wondered, does the missionary serve beyond the distribution of Bibles? As for the sacraments, such as "baptism, he did not see the necessity of ministers to perform it, since the Dissenters in England thought any other person might do it."[139] Who, after all, ordained John the Baptist? Likely Daniel Little frequently heard such comments, perhaps even asked such questions himself. In light of his failure to convert the Penobscots to the English language and customs and Protestantism, he doubtless wondered if Mr. Dexter, and others like him, had a point.

One of Little's close friends in the clergy, Jeremy Belknap, himself a missionary, had many such doubts, asked similar questions. He thought long and hard about the nature

---

[139] As quoted by Jeremy Belknap in his *Interleaved Almanac for 1788*, Belknap Papers, MHS.

of conversion from one belief to another, and thought that the task of the missionary, especially to the Indians, was herculean. Belknap had become interested in missionary work about the same time as Daniel Little, inspired as well, perhaps, by the examples of noteworthy messengers to the Indians active in New York, Connecticut, Massachusetts, and New Hampshire. Samuel Kirkland, Eleazar Wheelock, Gideon Hawley, and others, served as examples of missionaries who attempted to convert various tribes of the Iroquois and Algonquian Indians. Kirkland, for example, who had attended Eleazar Wheelock's Indian school in Lebanon, Connecticut, served as a missionary with the Iroquois of New York. A missionary with the Scots Society for Propagating Christian Knowledge, Kirkland learned the different dialects of the Six Nations and lived among the Iroquois before and after the American War for Independence. Belknap, who came to know Kirkland, reported an instance in 1772 during which a chief of the Oneida tribe complained of the "difficulties attending the Gospel among the Indians," telling Kirkland: "We are derided by our brothers . . . on acct of our X [Christian] profession. Time was when we were esteemed . . . and important in the Confederacy, as any others, but now we are looked upon as small things, or rather nothing at all." Years later, after Belknap had journeyed to upstate New York to visit the Oneida tribe, he understood more fully the situation in which American Indians often found themselves. His studies and experiences informed him that even among sophisticated people who have had the benefits of education, some refuse to give up some liberties for the good of the whole or to preserve the most important liberties. And people who are set in their ways and guided by custom and tradition do not easily change. English manners and habits often disgusted and repelled Indians. There were many examples of Indian youths who were taken from their tribe and educated among whites who constantly reminded the youth of their differences and supposed inferiority. At the same time, because of white influence, the youth is in the eyes of members of the tribe now different and in their eyes inferior. He is caught between two worlds and cannot quite become part of the former or return to the latter. Often they turned to drink in frustration. Daniel Little had firsthand experience of this two-world phenomenon, of a person caught between two different traditions and cultures, when he met and conversed with the Penobscot, Persock, in 1774.[140]

Little had been faced with the intransigence of the Penobscots, who were led by wise and experienced sachems who understood that treaties with the English represented a two-edged sword. "Where the white man puts down his foot, he never takes it up again," an Indian sachem once said. Another of Daniel Little's acquaintances, missionary Jedidiah Morse, many years later captured perfectly the situation in which the Penobscots found themselves in 1788:

The hunting grounds of the Indians on our frontiers are explored in all directions, by enterprizing white people. Their best lands are selected, settled, and at length, by treaty purchased. Their game is either wholly destroyed, or so diminished, as not to

---

[140] Kirkland, Samuel. *The Journals of Samuel Kirkland: 18th Century Missionary to the Iroquois, Government Agent, Father of Hamilton College.* New York: Hamilton College, 1980; Jeremy Belknap, Memorandum Book, Belknap Papers, MHS.

yield an adequate support. The poor Indians, thus deprived of their accustomed means of subsistence, and of what, in their own view, can alone render them respectable, as well as comfortable, are constrained to leave their homes, their goodly lands, and the sepulchres of their fathers, and either to go back into new and less valuable wildernesses, and to mingle with other tribes, dependant on their hospitality for a meagre support; or, without the common aids of education, to change at once all of their habits and modes of life; to remain on a pittance of the lands they once owned, which they know not how to cultivate, and to which they have not a complete title: In these circumstances they become insulated among those who despise them as an inferior race, fit companions of those only, who have the capacity and the disposition to corrupt them. In this degraded, most disconsolate, and heart sinking of all situations in which man can be placed, they are left miserably to waste away for a few generations, and then to become extinct forever!

The Penobscots had benefitted sufficiently from the French Catholics that there seemed to be little reason to abandon their teachings and traditions. As Captain Park Holland, who had served as surveyor in the Penobscot valley and who traveled briefly with Jeremy Belknap on his journey to Oneida New York in 1796, recalled, Catholicism had been largely successful in converting and instilling Christian habits in the Penobscot people.[141]

After Daniel Little's journey to the Penobscot region in 1788, he refrained from missionary journeys for several years, though his interests in promoting the work of

---

[141] Jedidiah Morse, *A Report to the Secretary of War of the United States on Indian Affairs* (New Haven, C.T.: S. Converse, 1822), 65-66; Belknap, *Journal of a Tour*, 6.

missionaries and establishing Christian ministers in the eastern frontier continued unabated. He corresponded with fellow clergymen, including members of the Society for Propagating of the Gospel, as well as statesmen and land speculators, about the work of converting the people of Maine and establishing viable churches in frontier communities. Little corresponded with General Henry Knox, who had a primary interest in the Waldo Patent, about the ministerial and missionary needs of the people who lived in this massive land grant along the northeast coast. In June 1789, Little wrote Knox that he had been recently at Portland conversing with Isaac Winslow, who had married into the Waldo family. Little had suggested "a Pattentee Missionary, a Man of true Science and Virtue," an idea that "has met with the Approbation of all who wish prosperity to the Pattentees, a reformation of manners among the present Settlers, and felicity to after generations." Knox supported the idea, but even more, wished to see established "a liberal School for the better Education of the more promising Youth." Little's sanguinity about the Waldo Patent, at least in his letter to Knox, was exuberant. "The Climate, the goodness of the Soil, the Extent of the Pattent, (equal to the whole State of Rhode Island) and the remotest part of it not more than 20 miles from Navigation, must in the name of Reason and Prophecy, make, by and by, a joyful Seat of Wealth, Honour, and Happiness, in the East." Patriot and optimist, he continued: "Mine Hairs are grey, and mine Eyes will only See the dawnings of American glory; but my prayer shall be that you, Sir, may live to see happiness forced like the rays of the rising Sun, and in particular may live to behold the happy effects of your generous purposes, in a large increase of knowledge and Virtue among the People of the eastern Shoars; and that they and their Children may feel the happy Effects of their own industry, Economy, temperance, and Brotherly Love."[142]

Knox responded to Little in October, supporting wholeheartedly Little's opinions, to which Little responded in kind in December, reinforcing his support for a special missionary to the Waldo Patent, and providing a portrait, based on his own experiences during the previous fifteen years, of what the duties and character of such a missionary would necessarily be. The missionary would have to divide his time between settled communities, helping them to establish a secure congregation of believers for which they would need to hire a resident clergyman, and newer settlements, which would require the most attention, as these people would be unused to the forms of religion, and require the most basic services, such as baptism. The missionary would have to adaptable, frugal, hospitable, virtuous, and an intellectual—"a man of Science." Little envisioned someone who would take his place in the work of ministering to the people of the Penobscot region: "He must necessarily be so much from his stated Home in visiting the settlement in the several parts of the Patent, which now line the Shore on the Bay and River Penobscot more than fifty miles, besides those in the more interiour parts of the Territory, that very little can be done for his support by his own attention to secular business, consistent with fidelity to the duties of the Office." Little believed that the establishment of secure

---

[142] Daniel Little to Henry Knox, 6/8/1789, Henry Knox Papers, Gilder Lehman Collection, New York Historical Society.

Christian settlements was required for the continuation of "American Glory" on the eastern frontier. "I thank you dear Sir for putting it in my way at the close of Life to add new wishes for the Happiness of the Eastern Territory where I have in my best days spent the cream of three Summers."[143]

The knowledge that Little had acquired on his many trips to the Penobscot region made him an important source of information for government and charitable institutions. The Society for Propagating the Gospel, in particular, relied on Little's observations and judgment in formulating plans for how to fulfill the Great Commission on the eastern frontier. Little wrote an extensive epistle in November, 1790, to Peter Thacher, Secretary of the Society, which Thacher published in a circular that was widely distributed to concerned parties. Little provided a sobering account of the state of affairs in the District of Maine. There is, he reported, a great number of people who live in "almost . . . total ignorance of God and religion. Few of them are taught to read, and those who have been taught, cannot now procure books. Many families have not had a bible or a testament in their houses for years past, and such is their poverty as to forbid their purchasing them. Many of them have lost their reverence for the Lord's day, and are strangers to religious institutions. Their children are educated not only in an ignorance of religion, but also without human learning, or even the arts of civilization. As a necessary consequence of this, crimes of the most attrocious [sic] nature, and such as naturally arise from a state of barbarism, have encreased among them, and

---

[143] Daniel Little to Henry Knox, 12/15/1789, Henry Knox Papers, Gilder Lehman Collection, New York Historical Society.

furnished large, but disagreeable business to the courts of law." Clearly, something had to be done.[144]

The causes of the state of affairs in the eastern frontier, according to Little, included "repeated Indian wars, for more than half a century, from their first settlement," which "obliged the people often to croud [sic] into forts and garrisons for safety; with little distinction of families and without proper means of education or religion. And there are to this day, observable in some places, the bad effects of garrison education." At the same time, itinerant preachers moved from place to place, providing services gratis, which prejudiced the people against more learned, ordained ministers who required a salary. The contempt of an established ministry prevented an orderly focus on literature and learning, which encouraged the illiterate and ignorant, and according to Little, a "mammonian, sectarian enthusiastic spirit." As a result, "many towns of sufficient ability for the support of the gospel, are weakned [sic] and at present rendered incapable of uniting in the choice of such ministers as they need, and which the happy few liberal and candid souls wish, men of knowledge, in whom are united wisdom, piety, integrity and Catholicism."[145]

Daniel Little in 1791 was sixty-seven years old; he perceived that his life was coming to a close, and that he would spend his remaining years serving his parish at Kennebunk, resting from the difficult travels he had pursued when a slightly younger man during the previous seventeen

---

[144] "A brief Account of the present State of the Society for propagating the Gospel."

[145] Ibid.

years. Then at the beginning of 1791, he received a letter from the Secretary of the Society for Propagating the Gospel, Peter Thacher, which changed everything. "Ever since my last Tour, as Missionary," Little wrote Thacher on March 28th, "I had given up the idea of ever leaving home again for the like purpose 'till I received your Letter . . . , the contents of which arrested my attention with deep concern to know Duty." The upshot of Thacher's letter was that the newly chartered Society for Propagating the Gospel sought to send missionaries into Maine, but the lack of remuneration, expense of time and energy, and danger in traveling, rendered it exceedingly difficult to recruit worthy men to journey on their behalf. Little's extensive response to Thacher is remarkable for its candor, wisdom, spirit of self-sacrifice, and extensive discussion of the characteristics and requirements of the missionary.[146]

Little's sense of duty toward the Great Commission, and his willingness to sacrifice domestic felicity for so great an object, is apparent in his letter to Thacher: "My domestic circumstances, for the last twelve month, have taken a new arrangement. My Son who presided in my former Absence, is removed from me, an aged and worthy consort with two amiable Daughters &c. are dependent upon my Care for their future Comfort." Besides family cares, his parish had not increased his salary over time, so that he was constantly engaged in "economical Saveing," with the consequence that it was a burden on "the Energy of the Mind" that is needed if he were to engage in "extensive and generous exertions."

---

[146] Daniel Little to Peter Thacher, 3/28/1791, Records of the Society for Propagating the Gospel Among the Indians and Others in North America, MHS..

Further, the "habitual cheerfulness and Serenity of mind" that was a consequence of "unremitted health of Body" has "greatly abated for the 3 years past." Moreover, "I have been in the Ministry 40 years this month, and now lack but 3 years and a few months of 70 years of Age." Family, money, health, and age: these were heavy burdens, indeed, on a person who is now being asked to engage in another arduous journey to the eastern frontier. But Little was up to it! The question was, would the parish agree. He posed the question to the parish, and asked the parishioners to give it some thought over the course of a week, then to give him their assent or denial. They agreed, sort of, voting to "leave the matter (to use their own expression) to me and Providence." That settled it. Little realized that the concerns of "flesh and blood" and such circumstances upon which our present life and it[s] comforts depend" have to be balanced with larger aims of importance and "the Voice of the public and the united Voice of our pious friends to whom we are intimately known." In addition, "the propogation [sic] of Christian knowledge and Virtue, among the sons [of] men, by every laudable moment in our power, is an imployment very acceptable to God and justly presents a first Choice to every Man. For a Belief of this, shall I not once more reapply the Apostolic Charge—'Go preach my Gospel to every Creature, and into whatsoever House ye enter first say Peace be to this House'." In short, Little believed that Providence called him forth again. To prepare, Little for the next few months "shall adjust my home affairs, so as to feel myself detached from every matter foreign to the Mission, that my Mind may be absorbed by the Object, which is necessary both for Comfort and Usefulness." Little had felt the effects of "divine

Wisdom and goodness" during his "former Endeavours," which called for "humility and thankfulness. But if I should, be, at this time, called only to be a weeping Prophet," that is, if his missionary journey should be filled with difficulties and suffering, "I hope for Submission with Reverence to the divine will, and by Heaven's assistance, never to desert the Cause of our gracious Master, in the most trying Hour."[147]

The men of the Society for Propagating of the Gospel asked Little for his opinion of what books to bring to the people of the eastern frontier. His response shows the kind of books that were on the top of his own reading list. "The Books I formerly distributed in the Penobscot Country (where I have heretofore chiefly officiated) were mostly of those published by the Society for promoting religious knowledge among the poor," an organization formed by Dissenters to the Church of England in 1750; their aim was to publish and distribute Bibles and other religious tracts that focused on the same goals that Little had, to promote good pious lives notwithstanding the particulars of religious belief. Besides the Bible, Little liked the works and hymns by Dr. Isaac Watts and other such "Plain tracts upon the importance of religion, to every Man's Comfort and Usefulness" as well as "Discourses upon the Duty and Priviledges [sic] of Public Worship," "Biographical Tracts with pious remarks upon Providential Events," works on "industry, temperance and economy, in the mode of Aphorisms or dialogues," but also "not forgetting the old New-England Primmer." Little believed that books should be "of little Bulk because more portable, sooner read and

---

[147] Ibid.

because of a greater diffusion of knowledge."[148]

Little's previous journeys to the Penobscot having taught him there were so many people hungry for religion, and so many communities yearning to form religious societies, and at the same time such a dearth of "learned and worthy" candidates, such that in some places the people were desperate for pastoral relief, that he suggested that he journey south before he journeyed north. He wondered, "whether it would not be my Duty, previous to my entering on the Mission, to journey through the Country at least as far as Cambridge and Boston, to acquaint my self personally with Candidates to inform them of and invite their attention to the eastern Country that when I am upon the Spot I may be able to recommend them, and by letter introduce them to the People, and in my absence for this purpose whether I may not Supply my own Pulpit a Sab[bath] or 2, as their [sic] may be occation [sic], at the expence of the Society." Speaking of expenses, Little discussed the rate of pay of missionaries, arguing justly that a person with dependents should be paid more than a single person. His own rate of pay in 1788 was "£80 for Six months, just double the Sum of my nominal Sallary at Home," which was just, as "the cares and Services of the Mission are also double, besides preparatory and currant expences." Little wrote parenthetically, "I covet no man's silver or gold. I envy no man's happiness." This, he implied, must be the missionary's mantra. The missionary should never appear dependent upon the people to whom they minister, which "will dishonour the Man and the

---

[148] Ibid. Isabel Rivers, "The First Evangelical Tract Society," *The Historical Journal* 50(2007): 1-22.

Christian." The aim of the missionary must be, rather, to accomplish "deeds of kindness to the Silent poor and afflicted, which will give him the Sublimest Pleasure and entitle him to hear those kind and condescending word[s] from his Master at the last Day. For as much as ye have done it unto one of the least of these my Bre[thre]n, yet have done it unto me."[149]

The Society for Propagating the Gospel asked Little to consider nominating a companion in missionary labor, a "young Gentleman with whom I have sufficient personal Knowledge to recommend, as a Man of benignity of Temper, chaste in his deportment, warmed with pious Zeal, able & apt to teach." Little was not willing to nominate anyone, such as his companion, on his previous journey, Abiel Abbot, but left it to the decision of the Society.[150]

The Society decided to send Little on his missionary journey accompanied by Abiel Abbot as well as an older man, the Rev. James Lyon, who served a parish at Machias, Maine. Lyon had lived for a time in Nova Scotia, where he served as a Presbyterian minister, had been an ardent patriot during the Revolutionary War, and had preached at Machias since 1771. If Little kept a journal of his 1791 journey, it is lost. Historical snippets inform us that he followed approximately the same route he and Abbot had taken in 1787. The three men journeyed over the course of three months in the summer, traveling through the counties of York, Cumberland, and Lincoln northeast to the Penobscot region. An antiquarian record from Augusta placed Little at

---

[149] Little to Thacher, 3/28/1791, MHS.

[150] Ibid.

Dr Daniel Cony's during the summer of 1791. "We gave Father Little fine strawberries and milk," the family recalled, "smoked salmon, smoked herring, baked beans, stewed peas, roasted potatoes, spruce beer, &c., &c., and Mr. Little, agreeably to Luke 8th, 'eat and drank such things as were set before him'." Another antiquarian record records that the people of the Maine frontier provided a hearty welcome to the elderly, apostolic-like Little. People gathered about and hung on his words. He preached "pardon and peace to the humble and penitent, he comforted the broken-hearted, and gave spiritual food to all who were hungering and thirsting after righteousness." "His preaching was like the mild and gracious doctrines of him who spake in the Father's name, and invited his erring, wandering children to return unto him, that they might be blest. While he taught them to fear offending a holy God, he also displayed his parental character, and urged upon their ingenuous minds the consideration of the love of God, and the compassion of Jesus Christ, who came to seek and to save those who were lost."[151]

Perhaps this describes the sentiments of the settlers who lived ten miles up the Sebasticook River from its confluence with the Kennebec. Little "spent Several Days among the people" in a land of "numerous" streams "that empty into Sebastacook." Little engaged in scientific pursuits at the same time that he performed his ministerial labors. In his

---

[151] *Bangor Historical Magazine*, 3(1887-1888): 209-210; James W. North, *A History of Augusta from the Earliest Settlement to the Present Time* (Augusta: Clapp and North, 1870), 236; John O. Choules and Thomas Smith, *The Origin and History of Missions*, 2 vols (Boston: Gould, Kendall and Lincoln, 1937): 2: 570-571.

correspondence with General Lincoln about the habits of fish, Lincoln had suggested that fish in Maine rivers return to the spot of their birth to spawn. Little thought about this at length, considered what he had observed, and could not think of an alternative argument. Indeed, while at Sebasticook the settlers informed him that "at the time for the running of the smaller fish they ascend the different streams at distinct Periods, in Succession. And that the Schulls [schools] never separate, interfere or transgress in their way to their respective Ponds or Lakes."[152]

As in 1787, when he journeyed with Abiel Abbot, Little's 1791 missionary endeavors concluded with visiting "most of the new towns and Plantations in the County of York"; again, he cut short this journey due to "the Season being so far advanced"; he "found it expedient to return Home leaving the 2 last Sab[bath]s of our Appointment to be given to the People at some future more favourable Season." Little, home a fortnight, was still recovering from "near 4 month unremitted attention to one important pleasing object." Meanwhile, he awaited a visit from his "worthy associate" Abiel Abbot so that they might provide a full transaction of their journey to the Society for Propagating the Gospel.[153]

At the same time he had occasion, the first Sabbath in November, to visit the town of Waterboro in York County, which had existed since before the war. Here Little visited the local parish, where he met some recent arrivals to the area from the Cocheco Valley. This was Jeremy Belknap's

---

[152] Daniel Little to Jeremy Belknap, 12/13/1791, Belknap Papers, MHS.

[153] Daniel Little to Jeremy Belknap, 11/11/1791, Belknap Papers, MHS.

territory, and sure enough, Little met some of Belknap's former parishioners, who spoke highly of their former pastor and his literary works. Belknap had donated books for their perusal, one of which was a sermon published in 1779 during the war, *Jesus Christ: The Only Foundation*. At Waterboro, Little "had the first reading of your Sermon," in which Belknap wrote: "We should always be sure that we pay more regard to the Truth itself, than to the sudden and extraordinary manner of its coming into our mind." "If we regard sudden impressions, tho' made in the very words of scripture, as a sign of the distinguishing favour of God toward us, and make use of them, to uphold a notion that we are admitted to more intimate communion with him, than other persons, who take pains to search the scripture, and acquire their knowledge more slowly and regularly; we have sad proof of the blinding power of spiritual aids and presumption." Conversion, Belknap argued, is based on slow growth toward truth not a sudden change. Little realized how significant this message was, a cautionary for the missionary who sought quick, unrealistic results. "If reprinted with some additions," Little wrote Belknap, "and scatter'd thro' the eastern district [it] would have a tendency to demolish many Sandy foundations and extinguish the many unhallowed flashes, kindled by the wood, hay and Stubble, of which the wilds of the east abound through the unseen wiles of the Devel [sic]." In other words, the quick and easy conversion taught by so many enthusiastic preachers and even respected Catholic priests would have a counter in the reality of true religious change. Little wrote to Peter Thacher, the Secretary of the Society for Propagating the Gospel, to arrange, if possible, for a reprinting of

Belknap's sermon.[154]

After his 1791 journey, Little retired from active missionary work. He began to enjoy more time with his wife and daughters, spending summers in a house he built around 1790 south of Kennebunk on the road between Wells and Sanford. Meanwhile he gave up a claim for "income of the Parish lands" in return for a cash payment of twenty pounds so that he could purchase a chaise. His wife was suffering more from illness and Little thought such an extravagance might help her when they went to town or church. The meetinghouse had by this time been relocated from the Landing, where Little lived, to the town center of Kennebunk, about two miles away. The Penobscot region, as well as other parts of the eastern frontier, were, Little thought, in the good hands of the Society for Propagating the Gospel. Abiel Abbot, for example, served the Penobscot region at Castine from 1793 to 1795. Although Little was no longer making missionary journeys, he kept abreast of missionary work in the district of Maine. During the winter of 1791-92, he penned Belknap a long epistle describing the state of Christianity in Maine. He noted the number of Congregational parishes and their ministers, the "old Churches vacant" in Lincoln County—there were eight--, and "towns supposed to be able to Support a Minister but have never hand any—there were nine such places, which showed the amount of work that remained to be done. Little estimated "40 thousand Souls" not be "the proper objects of that Christian benevolence which the Gospel was designed

---

[154] Little to Belknap, 11/11/1791 and 2/17/1792, Belknap Papers, MHS; Jeremy Belknap, *Jesus Christ, The Only Foundation* (Portsmouth, NH: Daniel Fowle, 1779).

to inspire and propagate." Little thought to provide the "Reasons why so many old Churches remain vacant" for Belknap, who was involved in the Society for Propagating the Gospel and Scots Society for Propagating Christian Knowledge. There were five reasons:

1. *Immoral & uninformed Conduct of some who have been in the ministerial Office.*
2. *Illiterate Teachers, of narrow party Spirit, who to establish themselves have offered their Service gratis.*
3. *A general prejudice against a regular & learned Ministry.*
4. *Many persons of a different persuasions from ye Churches in general—who if united and candid would be able to pursue public generous measures.*
5. *Long neglect of many people to attend public worship in any form whatsoever.*[155]

At the same time, however, the work of missionaries such as Daniel Little had mitigated some of the errors and ignorance among the people of the district of Maine. Many towns had reserve lands that could attract new settlers, which with increased population would enable towns to support an established clergyman. There were, moreover, numerous benevolent people willing "to take up the cross cheerfully and to find an Asylum in the lonely dwellings of the poor and to give them instruction, from the Word and Works of God." The vast wilderness of Maine ensured, Little thought, that "for many years to come" there would be frontier settlements that would require the services of a missionary. Little suggested that an established missionary work out of a

---

[155] Bourne, *History of Wells and Kennebunk*, 650, 661; Samuel A. Eliot, *Heralds of a Liberal Faith* vol. 2 (Boston, American Unitarian Association, 1910); "Mr. Little's acc[oun]t of Eastern towns," February 1, 1792, Belknap Papers, MHS.

"Central Situation, from whence to make Excursions abroad among the People, to receive and distribute Books, to direct and assist younger Missionaries and candidates." Perhaps aware that his script was difficult to decipher, Little added that "My pen is not easily governed when my tho'ts travel over the eastern World." "I am too old," he concluded melodramatically, "to make apologies for a dying Wish to throw my last mite into the evangelical Treasury."[156]

In these waning years of life, reflecting on the past and his experiences among the Penobscot Indians, Little wished that such organizations as the Massachusetts Historical Society, founded by Jeremy Belknap in 1791 and dedicated to preserving the records of the human and natural past, might find the means to preserve the history, traditions, and language of the Penobscot tribe. The justification for such preservation was obvious, as they are "one of the most antient and venerable, on the eastern shore, and the only Tribe now existing in that part of the Commonwealth, that a more full information might be obtained and preserved, of their former and present State with respect to their Numbers, Wars, alliances, treaties, their civil and military Government, their antient religion, and when they embraced Christianity; their mode of living and dying, their Language, its construction and extent." Little himself had been involved in transcribing portions of their language into the Lord's Prayer, and preserving basic words, such as their words counting from 1 to 20. Such information "would be a Curiosity in a future Day, and perhaps help us to ascertain, with greater precision, when, and from what part of the old

---

[156] "Little's Account of Eastern Towns," and Little to Belknap, 2/17/1792, MHS.

World, they originated."[157] Religious thinkers and other intellectuals had for many years sought to explain the origins of the Indians in America: whether they were descendants of northern Europeans, descendants of the Hebrews, people who crossed the sea from the Old World at some ancient date, or migrated across land from northeastern Asia thousands of years before.

In 1798, Rev. Caleb Bradley of Portland, traveling through Kennebunk, stopped at Daniel Little's house at Kennebunk Landing. In his diary, Bradley said that Little was "a man of a thousand," and that "Kennebunk is a beautiful place, and Mr. Little has one of the most beautiful ministerial situations I ever saw. He has a very convenient house, a fine garden, through the middle of which a small brook meanders, and in the summer seasons, in the morning, a person may divert himself by catching salmon trout." One gathers in looking over the scattered records and anecdotes of Little's final years that he lived with pleasant memories of a life well-lived. His work as a missionary in the Penobscot region was a highlight. "I review the time I spent in the eastern country, with more pleasure than any other part of my life of equal duration, though I most devoutly wished to have served them better, and that the serious and sacred instruction of the gospel had been crowned with extensive and general blessings." Little's sometimes public comments deriding the continued difficulties of the Gospel on the Eastern Frontier belied the fact that he felt true affection for these people:

I feel myself indebted to the eastern people, for a thousand

---

[157] Little to Belknap, 4/5/1793, MHS.

tokens of civil and religious affection. And from the feelings of a father and friend, I may at this late period of life, in some respect, have been partial in my judgment. But if I find a disposition to apoligize [sic] for some of their misfortunes, . . . I trust it will be excused. Pray what could be expected of a country harassed by indian . . . wars at different times, for near a century, remote from the happy influence of stated religious instruction, and the center of which, even to this day, is 150 miles from any public seminary of learning, and lesser means of education, difficult to obtain? Indeed I have been surprised to find the people in general so hospitable and so well informed; and so many respectable characters in the literary line, though but very few compared with what the great number of the people and the extent of the country require, for their rising happiness and honor.[158]

Little felt blessed as well with the longstanding benevolent relationship he had with his Kennebunk parishioners. "I have been witness to the generous exertions of a small parish, in the eastern district, near 40 years ago, consisting of but 30 families, all united as a band of brothers in the settlement and support of a minister, none rich; none complained of being burdened; all submitted chearfelly [sic] to an equal division of aid, according to their respective abilities. They now exist in harmony with their first pastor, and with the addition of five times their first number." The parish at Kennebunk had avoided what had often occurred to parishes throughout New England: "the bitter and indiscreet zeal of some high professors of religion, and the equally indiscreet zeal of their opposers; together with the redicule

---

[158] Bourne, *History of Wells and Kennebunk*, 651; "Little's Account of Eastern Towns," MHS.

[sic] and reproach, with which all serious religion is treated by too many, have conspired to lessen the credit of that glorious gospel." The result was that Kennebunk had "a happy meeting in religious duties" and a "strength and beauty of society."[159]

The year after Bradley's visit and enthusiastic comments about Rev. Little's situation, the burden of time descended upon the 75-year-old pastor. In 1799, infirmities of body or mind prevented Little from carrying out the functions of his office. The parish had already seen this coming—perhaps Little had been in decline for several years—as in April, 1796, the Kennebunk parish voted "that further supplies in the Pulpit was necessary." During 1799, guest preachers served in the pulpit. One young man was invited but refused, then another, Nathaniel Fletcher, accepted, and became associate minister in 1800. At the ordination in September, 1800, Little was too ill to participate. During the next year, he had some good days where he could participate, though the parish was now in the hands of Rev. Fletcher. On October 3rd, 1801, Little was struck with paralysis, and died the next day. "When he rose in the morning . . . he complained of a pain in his stomach. He sat however at the table with his family at breakfast, but could not take his breakfast with them; and said his pain increased. . . . Sitting in his chair, he leaned his head back, spread his handkerchief before his face, and spake no more."[160]

---

[159] "Little's Account of Eastern Towns," MHS.

[160] Bourne, *History of Kennebunk and Wells*, 628, 631, 722; Records of the First Parish; Shipton, *Harvard Graduates*, 47.

The inscription over Rev. Daniel Little's grave was a worthy epitaph of his life's work:

Blessed are they who have turned many to righteousness.

Apostle of the East

SOURCES CONSULTED

Unpublished Manuscript Sources *(Used by Permission)*

Brick Store Museum, Kennebunk, Maine

Journals of Reverend Daniel Little (Kennebunk) (Miscellaneous Collection #23):

    Mr. Little's Journal from July 1, 1774 to October 10, 1774

    Mr. Little's Tour of the White Mountains (1784)

    Journal of Mr. Little's Tour to Penobscot, 1786

    Extracts from the Rev. Daniel Little's Journal of 1787

    Mr. Little's Tour to Penobscot by Direction of the Governor & Council from June 3 to July 15, 1788.

Account of the Tour & Mission of the Rev. Mr. Little in Company with the Rev. Abiel Abbot, in the year 1787.

Commissioners Conference with the Indians at Penobscot in 1786.

Subscriber's Account of Daniel's Little's Meeting with Penobscot Indians, June, 1788.

Massachusetts Historical Society

Daniel Little, "General Account of the Rise and Progress of the Eastern Mission By Letter to Honourable Samuel Phillips, Esq.", February 18, 1788, Miscellaneous Bound Manuscripts.

Daniel Little to Peter Thacher, March 28, 1791, Records of the Society for Propagating the Gospel Among the Indians and Others in North America.

Daniel Little to Jeremy Belknap, September 8, 1766, Belknap Papers.

Daniel Little to Jeremy Belknap, June 1784, Belknap Papers.

Daniel Little to Jeremy Belknap, August 10, 1785, Belknap Papers.

Daniel Little to Benjamin Stevens, August 15, 1785, Belknap Papers.

Daniel Little to Jeremy Belknap, November, 11, 1791, Belknap Papers.

Daniel Little to Jeremy Belknap, December 13, 1791, Belknap Papers.

Daniel Little to Jeremy Belknap, February 17, 1792: Includes "Account of the State of Religion in Churches in Maine," Belknap Papers.

Daniel Little, "Plan of the Penobscot River from the H[ea]d of the Tide to the H[eigh]t of Land taken from the Indians July 18, 1786," Belknap Papers.

"Mr. Little's acc[oun]t of Eastern towns," February 1, 1792, Belknap Papers.

"Minutes of the Progressive Growth and Maturity of the most useful Vegetables at Penobscot &c. with Some recreational observations in the year 1785 by the Rev[eren]d Mr. Little, while Missionary there," *Interleaved Almanac for 1788*, Belknap Papers.

Jeremy Belknap, Memorandum Book, Belknap Papers.

Daniel Little to Isaac Smith, September, 1785, Smith-Carter Family Papers.

Daniel Little to Jeremy Belknap, 4/5/1793, MHS Archives.

New York Historical Society

Daniel Little to Henry Knox, June 8, 1789, Henry Knox Papers, Gilder Lehrman Collection.

Daniel Little to Henry Knox, December 15, 1789, Henry Knox Papers, Gilder Lehrman Collection.

Maine Historical Society

Records of the First Parish Church of Kennebunk: including Records of Baptisms, Marriages, and Deaths, 1750-1890.

Rauner Library, Dartmouth College

Daniel Little to Sir William Pepperrell, May 25, 1758.

Published Contemporary Sources

A brief Account of the present State of the Society for propagating the Gospel among the Indians and Others in North-America,--with a Sketch of the Manner in which they mean to pursue the Objects of their Institution. Boston: Thomas Adams, 1791.

Acts and Resolves of the Commonwealth of Massachusetts, 1786-1787. Boston: Wright & Potter, 1893.

Alden, Timothy. *A Collection of American Epitaphs and Inscriptions.* New York: Marks, 1814.

Baxter, James P. Editor. *Documentary History of the State of Maine.* Volume Nineteen. Portland: Lefavor-Tower, Co., 1914.

Belknap, Jeremy. *Jesus Christ, The Only Foundation.* Portsmouth, NH: Daniel Fowle, 1779.

Belknap, Jeremy. "Tour to the White Mountains." Belknap Papers. *Collections of the Massachusetts Historical Society.* Series Five. Volume Two. Boston: Massachusetts Historical Society, 1877.

Brief Account of the Society for Propagating the Gospel Among the Indians and Others in North-America. Boston: 1798.

Cutler, William P. and Julia P. *Life, Journals, and Correspondence of the Rev. Manasseh Cutler, LL.D.* Two Volumes. Cincinnati: Robert Clarke & Co., 1888.

Force, Peter. *American Archives*, 4th Series, III, 1840.

Greenleaf, Jonathan. *Sketches of the Ecclesiastical History of the State of Maine.* Portsmouth, NH: Harrison Gray, 1821.

Kirkland, Samuel. *The Journals of Samuel Kirkland: 18th Century Missionary to the Iroquois, Government Agent, Father of Hamilton College.* New York: Hamilton College, 1980.

Lewis, W. *The New Dispensatory.* London: Nourse, 1781.

Little, Daniel. "Observations upon the Art of making Steel." *Memoirs of the American Academy of Arts and Sciences*. 1(1783): 525-528.

Morse, Jedidiah. *A Report to the Secretary of War of the United States on Indian Affairs*. New Haven, C.T.: S. Converse, 1822.

"Strictures of the Life, &c. of the Rev. Daniel Little," *Piscataqua Evangelical Magazine*. Volume 2. 1806.

Sullivan, James. *The History of the District of Maine*. Boston: Thomas and Andrews, 1795.

"The Journal of the Rev. John Cleaveland." *Historical Collections of the Essex Institute*. 12(1874): 92-94.

Whipple, Joseph. *The History of Acadie, Penobscot Bay and River*. Bangor, ME: Peter Edes, 1816.

Secondary Sources

America: A Catholic Review of the Week 26 (1921-1922).

Bangor Historical Magazine. 1(1886), 3(1887-1888), 4(1889), 5(1889-1990).

Banks, Charles E. *History of York, Maine*. Volume Two. Boston: 1931, 1935; reprint Baltimore: Regional Publishing Co., 1967.

Beaver, R. Pierce. Editor. *American Missions in Bicentennial Perspective*. South Pasadena, CA: American Society of Missiology, 1977.

Boucher Olivia, and Melissa L. Olson. *Isleboro—An Island in Penobscot Bay*: http://islesboro.mainememory.net/page/1049/display.html

Bourne, Edward E. *The History of Wells and Kennebunk*. Portland, ME: B. Thurston & Co., 1875.

Briggs, L. Vernon. *History of Shipbuilding on North River, Plymouth County, Massachusetts*. Boston: Coburn Brothers, 1889.

Calloway, Colin G. *The American Revolution in Indian Country: Crisis and Diversity in Native American Communities*. Cambridge: Cambridge University Press, 1995.

Candage, R. G. F. *Historical Sketch of Bluehill, Maine*. Ellsworth, ME:

Hancock County Publishing Co., 1905.

Chaney, Charles L. *The Birth of Missions in America.* Eugene, OR: Wipf & Stock, 2012.

Chase George W. *The History of Haverhill, Massachusetts, from its first settlement in 1640, to the Year 1860.* Haverhill, MA: By the author, 1861.

Choules John O., and Thomas Smith. *The Origin and History of Missions.* Two Volumes. Boston: Gould, Kendall and Lincoln, 1937.

Clayton, W. Woodford. *History of York County, Maine.* Philadelphia: Everts & Peck, 1880.

Collections and Proceedings of the Maine Historical Society. Second Series. Volume Four. Portland: Maine Historical Society, 1893.

Coolidge Austin J., and John B. Mansfield. *A History and Description of New England, General and Local.* Volume One. Boston: Austin Coolidge, 1859.

Currier, John J. *History of Newbury, Massachusetts, 1635-1902.* Newbury, MA: Damrell and Upham, 1902.

Dean, Benjamin A. *Annals of the Brentwood, N. H. Congregational Church and Parish.* Boston: T. W. Ripley, 1889.

Eckstorm, Fannie Hardy. "History of the Chadwick Survey from Fort Pownal in the District of Maine to the Province of Quebec in Canada in 1764." *Sprague's Journal of Main History* 14(1926): 63-89.

Eliot, Samuel A. *Heralds of a Liberal Faith.* Volume Two. Boston, American Unitarian Association, 1910.

Farrow, John P. *History of Islesborough, Maine.* Bangor, ME: Burr, 1893.

Godfrey, John E. "The Ancient Penobscot, or Panawanskek." *The Historical Magazine*, 1872: http://cprr.org/Museum/BMLRR/Penobscot.html.

Helmreich, Jonathan E. *Eternal Hope: The Life of Timothy Alden, Jr.* Cranbury, NJ: Cornwall Books, 2001.

History of Penobscot County. Cleveland: Williams, Chase & Co., 1882.

Hosmer, George L. *An Historical Sketch of the Town of Deer Isle,*

Maine. Boston: Stanley and Usher, 1886.

Lagerborn, Charles H. "Tested Loyalties and Sense of Obligation: Two Maine Men and the American Revolution. *Journal of the American Revolution.* September, 2017: https://allthingsliberty.com/2017/09/tested-loyalties-sense-obligation-two-maine-men-american-revolution/

Lawson, Russell M. *Passaconaway's Realm: Captain John Evans and the Exploration of Mount Washington.* Hanover, NH: University Press of New England, 2002.

_____. *Portsmouth: An Old Town by the Sea.* Charleston, SC: Arcadia Publishing, 2003.

Locke, John L. *Sketches of the History of the Town of Camden, Maine.* Hallowell, ME: Master, Smith & Co., 1859.

Lord, Willis. *History of Waterboro*, 1987: http://www.waterboro-me.net/docs/information/history_waterboro.html

McLachlan, James. *Princetonians, 1748-1768: A Biographical Dictionary.* Princeton, NJ: Princeton University Press, 2015.

McLellan, Hugh E. *History of Gorham, Maine.* Portland, ME: Smith & Sale, 1903.

"Mount Desert Island: Shaped by Nature": http://mdi.mainememory.net/page/205/display.html.

Munson, Gorham B. *Penobscot: Down East Paradise.* Philadelphia: Lippincott, 1959.

North, James W. *A History of Augusta from the Earliest Settlement to the Present Time.* Augusta: Clapp and North, 1870.

Preble, George H. *Genealogical Sketch of the First Three Generations of Prebles in America.* Boston: David Clapp, 1868.

Report of the Select Committee of the Society for Propagating the Gospel among the Indians and Others in North America. Boston: John Wilson and Son, 1856.

Rivers, Isabel. "The First Evangelical Tract Society." *The Historical Journal* 50(2007).

Schmidt, Henrietta. "Apostle of the East." *Tourist News.* June 24, 1960.

Shipton, Clifford K. *Biographical Sketches of Those Who Attended Harvard College* (Sibley's Harvard Graduates) Volume Twelve.

Boston: Massachusetts Historical Society, 1962, 41-48.

Spalding George B. *Historical Discourse Delivered on the One Hundredth Anniversary of the Piscataqua Association of Ministers.* Dover, NH: Morning Star Job Printing Office, 1882.

Taylor, Alan. *Liberty Men and Great Proprietors: The Revolutionary Settlement on the Maine Frontier, 1760-1820.* Chapel Hill, NC: University of North Carolina Press, 1990.

The Register of the Officers and Members of the Society of Colonial Wars in the State of Maine. Portland: Marks Printing House, 1905.

Tortora, Daniel J. *Fort Halifax: Winslow's Historic Outpost.* Charlestown, SC: The History Press, 2014.

Varney, George J. *Gazetteer of the State of Maine.* Boston: B. B. Russell, 1881.

Waterman, Charles E. *The Maine Watermans.* Mechanic Falls, ME: Ledger Publishing Co., 1906.

Waterman, Rose B. *Maynard S. Bird: The Sage of a Maine Son.* Lincoln, NE: IUniverse, 2005.

Wheeler, George A. *History of Brunswick, Topsham, and Harpswell, Maine.* Brunswick, ME: Mudge, 1878.

——————————. *History of Castine, Penobscot, and Brooksville, Maine.* Bangor, ME: Burr & Robinson, 1875.

Williamson, William D. "Notice of Orono, Chief at Penobscot." *Collections of the Massachusetts Historical Society.* Third Series. Volume Nine. Boston: Little and Brown, 1846.

Apostle of the East

MAPS

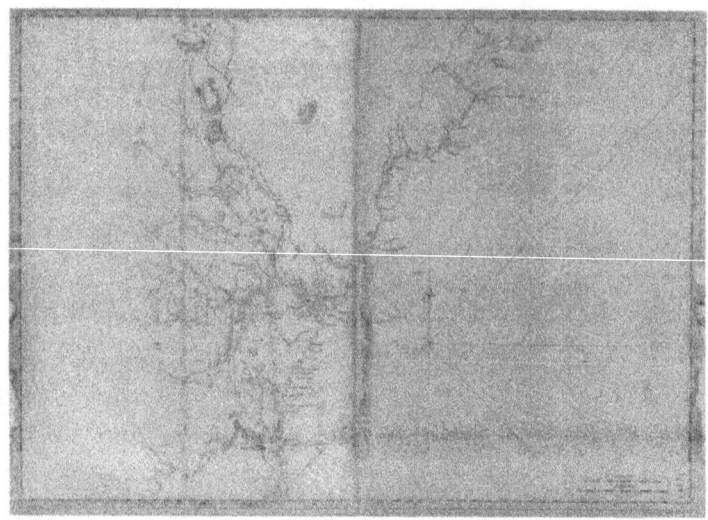

Coastal Maine with Kennebunk
Courtesy Library of Congress, Public Domain

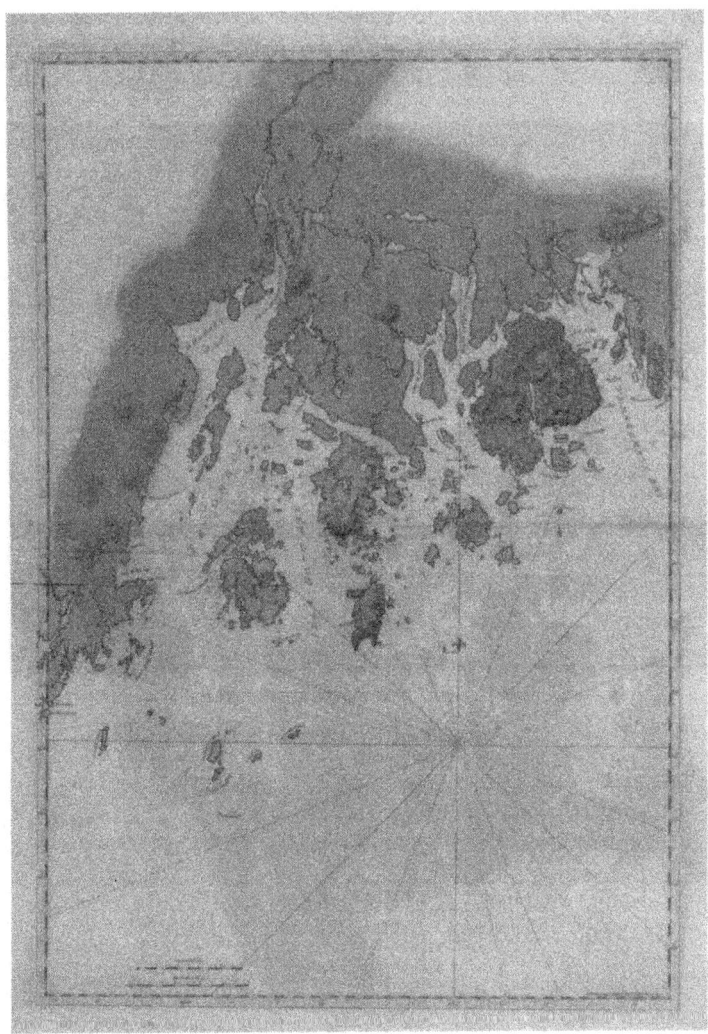

Penobscot Bay, Maine
Courtesy Library of Congress, Public Domain

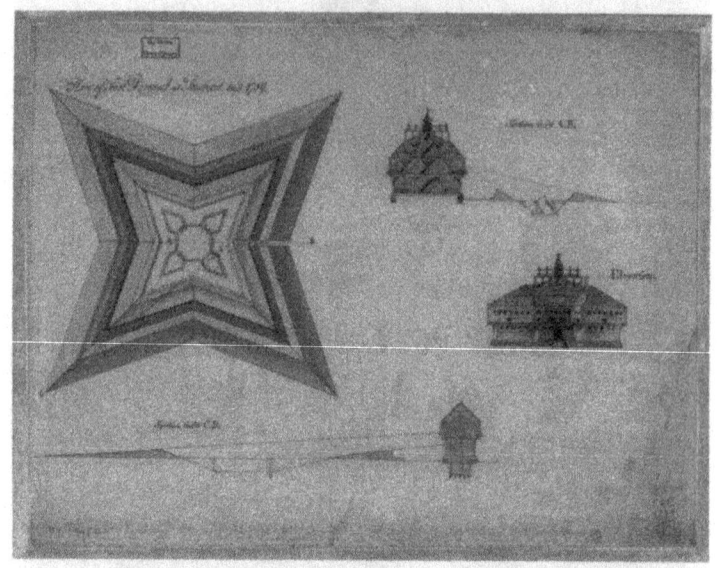

Plan of Fort Pownall, Maine
Courtesy Library of Congress, Public Domain

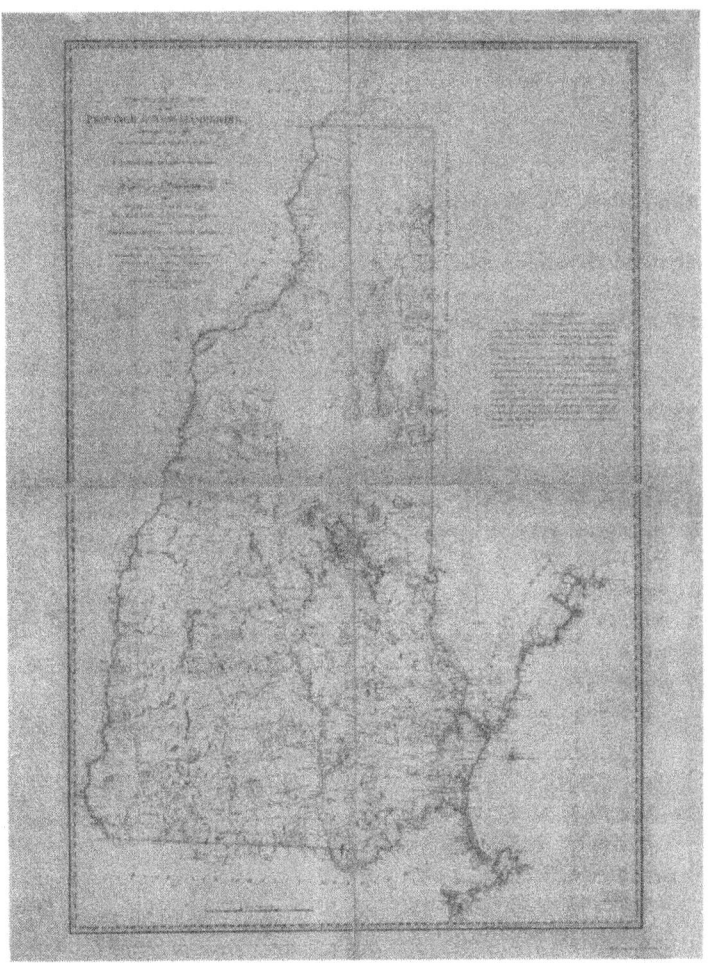

Map of New Hampshire
Courtesy Library of Congress, Public Domain

INDEX

A

Abbot, Abiel, 144, 146, 147, 148, 174, 176, 178, 184
Abenaki Indians, 2, 25, 34, 136, 145
Alden, Timothy, 21, 84, 141, 142, 186, 189
Alford, John, 122
Algonquian Indians, 5, 25, 112, 136, 163
American Academy of Arts and Sciences, 84, 85, 187
Androscoggin River, 70, 78, 87, 91, 94, 147, 159
Anglicanism, 26
Apostle Paul, 29, 30
Arnold, Benedict, 77, 78, 79
Augusta, Maine, 78, 144, 174, 175, 189

B

Bagaduce River, 55, 57, 103, 113, 125, 126, 138, 145, 149, 157
Bangor, Maine, 49, 54, 55, 59, 65, 104, 111, 125, 129, 132, 136, 147, 149, 151, 175, 187, 189, 190
Battle of Bunker Hill, 73, 130
Belknap, Jeremy, 87, 88, 89, 90, 91, 93, 94, 95, 96, 99, 101, 102, 103, 112, 114, 116, 134, 135, 162, 164, 165, 176, 178, 179, 180, 181, 185, 186
Bernard, Francis, 49, 106, 107
Bertheamer, Moris, 135
Berthiaume, Juniper, 127, 128, 129, 130, 135, 137, 141, 156
Berwick, Maine, 14, 90
Blue Hill, Maine, 35, 46, 49, 51, 53, 54, 55, 57, 82, 113, 114, 145
Boston, Massachusetts, 13, 15, 19, 27, 33, 40, 53, 54, 66, 68, 69, 71, 72, 73, 74, 82, 96, 99, 117, 123, 128, 129, 131, 133, 135, 143, 149, 162, 173, 175, 179, 186, 187, 188, 189, 190
Bourne, Edward, vii, 13, 14, 16, 17, 18, 32, 68, 73, 84, 85, 137, 140, 179, 182, 183, 188
Brentwood, New Hampshire, 14, 15, 86, 188
Brewer, John, 58, 127, 130, 138, 146, 150, 151, 156, 158
Buck, Jonathan, 34, 58, 62, 127, 156
Bucksport, Maine, 58, 63, 107, 145, 156
Buxton, Maine, 19, 31, 32

C

Camden, Maine, 37, 64, 66, 67, 68, 102, 118, 139, 158, 189
Cape Elizabeth, 37, 74
Cary, Richard, 121, 141
Casco Bay, 37, 74, 75
Castine, Maine, 55, 56, 57, 58, 79, 81, 82, 103, 118, 125, 129, 131, 145, 149, 178, 190
Catholicism, 5, 6, 26, 28, 40, 61, 71, 105, 108, 110, 117, 121, 128, 130, 131, 135, 142, 145, 161, 165, 169, 177, 187
Chadwick, James, 58, 106, 107,

108, 109, 110, 188
Cocheco River, 90
Coercive Acts, 69, 71
Coffin, Paul, 31, 32
Colbourn, William, 132, 134, 136, 150, 156, 158
Congregationalism, 9, 17, 70, 137
Connecticut River, 87, 93, 94, 95, 109
Cutler, Manasseh, 89, 90, 91, 99, 101, 112, 186

D

Dartmouth (Jefferson), New Hampshire, 27, 94, 186
Deer Isle, 37, 49, 52, 53, 54, 55, 57, 82, 104, 113, 117, 118, 189
Dover, New Hampshire, 3, 34, 90, 95, 100, 190

E

Ellis River, 91
English, 5, 9, 24, 25, 26, 38, 41, 42, 55, 56, 58, 60, 61, 65, 69, 71, 77, 86, 88, 97, 104, 105, 106, 107, 108, 111, 117, 119, 121, 122, 127, 128, 130, 132, 133, 136, 138, 139, 141, 142, 144, 145, 162, 164
Evans, John, 89, 91, 92, 93, 189

F

Falmouth, Maine, 24, 26, 70, 72, 74, 75, 76, 82, 123
Fisher, Joshua, 89, 90, 91, 93
Fletcher, Nathaniel, 183
Fort Halifax, 78, 130, 190
Fort Pownall, 34, 57, 60, 62, 63, 106, 107, 110, 193
French, 2, 3, 5, 24, 25, 26, 28, 34, 40, 47, 58, 60, 71, 78, 105, 126, 128, 136, 138, 141, 142, 153, 165
French-Indian War, 2, 24, 26, 34, 39, 50, 51, 58, 71, 77, 78, 91, 105, 106, 108, 132

G

Gospel of Mark, 7, 14
Gospel of Matthew, 7, 14
Great Commission, 6, 7, 14, 29, 30, 33, 42, 71, 98, 143, 161, 168, 170
Gyles, John, 99

H

Hampstead, New Hampshire, 8, 10, 12, 14, 86
Hancock, John, 148, 188
Haverhill, Massachusetts, 1, 3, 8, 9, 10, 12, 14, 58, 86, 188
Hemmenway, Moses, 31

I

Iroquois Indians, 127, 163, 164, 187
Isleboro, Maine, 64, 103, 124, 139, 157, 187

K

Kenduskeag River, 59, 129, 137
Kennebec River, 25, 35, 37, 67, 69, 77, 78, 109, 123, 144, 158, 159
Kennebunk Landing, 27, 181
Kennebunk River, 1, 11, 16, 147
Kennebunk, Maine, iv, vii, 1, 5, 11, 13, 14, 16, 17, 18, 27, 28, 29, 31, 32, 35, 36, 68, 71, 73, 82, 84, 85, 92, 96, 99, 101, 102,

117, 122, 133, 137, 139, 140, 144, 147, 159, 169, 178, 179, 181, 182, 183, 184, 186, 188, 191
King George's War, 26
King Philip's War, 26
King William's War, 26
Kirkland, Samuel, 163, 164, 187
Kittery, Maine, 24, 26, 28, 34, 90, 101
Knox, Henry, 166, 167, 168, 185, 186

L

Lincoln, Benjamin, 68, 119, 130, 131, 152, 154, 174, 175, 176, 178, 188, 190
Little, Abiah Clement, 8
Little, Daniel Jr., i, ii, iv, v, 1, 2, 3, 4, 5, 6, 7, 8, 10, 11, 12, 13, 14, 16, 17, 18, 19, 20, 21, 22, 26, 27, 28, 29, 31, 32, 33, 34, 35, 36, 38, 40, 41, 42, 43, 44, 46, 47, 48, 49, 50, 51, 52, 53, 54, 55, 57, 60, 62, 63, 64, 65, 66, 67, 68, 69, 71, 73, 74, 80, 81, 82, 84, 85, 86, 87, 88, 89, 90, 91, 92, 94, 95, 96, 97, 99, 101, 102, 103, 104, 105, 106, 108, 110, 112, 113, 114, 116, 117, 118, 119, 121, 123, 124, 126, 127, 128, 129, 130, 131, 133, 135, 137, 138, 139, 140, 141, 142, 143, 144, 145, 146, 147, 148, 149, 150, 151, 152, 153, 155, 157, 158, 159, 160, 161, 162, 164, 165, 167, 168, 169, 170, 172, 173, 174, 175, 176, 178, 179, 180, 181, 182, 183, 184, 185, 186, 187, 190
as Apostle of the East, 4, 161
as missionary, v, 11, 20, 29, 30, 31, 33, 40, 42, 54, 55, 67, 68, 85, 87, 101, 102, 116, 117, 121, 141, 144, 148, 161, 165, 170, 172, 173, 174, 176, 177, 178, 179, 181
as pastor, 4, 5, 6, 11, 13, 14, 15, 16, 17, 20, 21, 37, 38, 48, 54, 82, 85, 102, 116, 149
as scientist, 6, 82, 85, 86, 88, 101
education of, 10, 11, 12
family of, 9, 18, 19, 21
journeys of, 1, 4, 6, 10, 11, 12, 27, 28, 29, 30, 31, 32, 35, 36, 41, 43, 45, 46, 47, 50, 52, 54, 56, 57, 60, 62, 63, 64, 66, 68, 69, 77, 79, 87, 88, 89, 90, 91, 94, 96, 99, 101, 102, 103, 104, 105, 106, 107, 108, 109, 110, 112, 116, 117, 119, 121, 123, 124, 126, 127, 130, 134, 138, 139, 144, 146, 147, 149, 150, 156, 158, 159, 160, 161, 163, 165, 170, 171, 173, 174, 176, 178
personality of, 20, 21, 22, 48, 53, 82, 140, 161
religious beliefs of, 6, 19, 21, 44, 48, 53, 56, 81, 82
youth of, 8, 9, 10
Little, Daniel Little, Sr., 8, 10, 11
Little, Mary Emerson, 18, 27
Little, Sarah Coffin, 19, 20
Louisburg, 26, 51
Lowder, Jonathan, 60, 128

M

Machias, Maine, 63, 74, 174
Maine, ii, iv, 1, 3, 5, 11, 12, 13,

14, 16, 17, 19, 24, 25, 26, 27,
28, 31, 32, 33, 34, 36, 38, 40,
48, 50, 54, 55, 58, 63, 65, 67,
68, 70, 71, 73, 74, 77, 78, 79,
81, 83, 86, 88, 92, 95, 99, 106,
109, 112, 128, 129, 133, 135,
136, 137, 144, 147, 148, 159,
166,168, 170, 174, 176, 178,
179, 184, 185, 186, 187, 188,
189, 190, 191, 192, 193
Marsh, John, 131, 135, 137
Massachusetts, 1, 3, 8, 9, 10, 12,
16, 18, 19, 26, 33, 34, 39, 49,
53, 58, 64, 72, 77, 80, 84, 86,
88, 95, 96, 100, 102, 106, 118,
122, 123, 127, 130, 131, 132,
133, 135, 136, 142, 143, 144,
147, 150, 152, 154, 156, 161,
163, 180, 184, 186, 188, 190
Massachusetts General Court, 16,
33, 34, 84, 123, 130, 135, 143
Mattawamkeag River, 110, 111,
133, 135
Megunticook River, 66, 67, 102
Merrimack River, 8, 10, 11, 61
Moody, Joseph, 12, 13, 14
Morse, Jedidiah, 164, 165, 187
Mount Desert Island, 42, 47, 48,
49, 51, 103, 189
Mount Katahdin, 99, 110
Mount Washington, 86, 87, 88, 91,
92, 93, 99, 100, 101, 112, 116,
189
Mousam River, 16, 147
Mowat, Henry, 75, 76

N

Naskeag Point, 37, 38, 49, 51, 52,
104, 113
New Hampshire, 3, 8, 9, 12, 14,
33, 34, 64, 81, 86, 88, 91, 95,
96, 99, 109, 144, 163, 194
Newburyport, Massachusetts, 1, 8,
10, 11, 12, 19, 77, 86
Noble, Seth, 54, 123, 129, 130,
136, 137, 151, 154, 156
Norridgewock Indians, 25, 79, 145

O

Old Town, Maine, 104, 105, 107,
108, 110, 113, 114, 117, 125,
126, 131, 132, 135, 137, 141,
146, 150, 151, 156, 189
Orono, 111, 126, 131, 133, 134,
135, 141, 142, 146, 152, 156,
190
Orson Neptune, 152
Ossipee River, 91, 96, 148

P

Pamola, 112
Passadumkeag River, 111, 126
Peabody River, 91, 94
Penobscot Indians, 25, 40, 59,
107, 121, 123, 130, 146, 151,
180, 184
Penobscot River, 11, 57, 60, 99,
104, 106, 109, 111, 112, 116,
119, 121, 122, 138, 145, 146,
151, 185
Pepperrell, William, 24, 26, 27,
28, 186
Persock, 60, 164
Phillips, Samuel, 33, 34, 35, 41,
143, 144, 185
phlogiston, 83, 84
Piscataqua River, 11, 14, 20, 24,
25, 90, 147
Piscataquis River, 109, 111, 133
Portsmouth, New Hampshire, 13,
14, 24, 86, 89, 94, 149, 178,
186, 187, 189

Pownalborough, Maine, 67, 69, 130, 147, 156, 157
Pownall, Thomas, 24, 26, 58
Preble, Jedidiah, 24, 27, 58, 106
Preble, John, 58, 60, 106, 108
Puritans, 9
Putnam, Israel, 130

Q

Quebec, 26, 27, 28, 61, 77, 78, 79, 105, 106, 108, 109, 126, 128, 188
Queen Anne's War, 26

R

Rice, Thomas, 123, 130, 139
Richardson, James, 42, 47, 48, 52
Rockport, Maine, 67, 102, 118, 124

S

Saco River, 11, 25, 31, 36, 89, 91, 94, 95, 147
Sebasticook River, 78, 130, 175
Second Parish of Wells, 5, 16, 71, 72
Sewall, Stephen, 10
Smith, Isaac, 102, 117, 118, 185
Society for Propagating the Gospel, 5, 122, 123, 142, 143, 144, 148, 162, 168, 170, 174, 176, 177, 178, 185, 186, 190
Sowadabscook River, 58, 104, 107
Squamscott River, 14
St. Francis Indians, 109, 128
St. John's River, 25
Stamp Act, 71
Stevens, Benjamin, 101, 113, 114, 116, 185

T

Tea Act, 71
Thacher, Peter, 168, 170, 174, 177, 185
Treat, Robert, 107, 129, 131, 134, 138, 146, 150, 153, 156

U

Union River, 36, 38, 40, 45, 46, 57, 104
Universalism, iv, 6

V

Vinalhaven, 37, 53

W

Waldo Patent, 64, 145, 166, 167
War for Independence, 5, 71, 74, 97, 128, 140, 163, 188, 189
Wells, Maine, vii, 5, 13, 14, 16, 17, 18, 31, 32, 33, 68, 71, 72, 73, 84, 85, 86, 88, 114, 122, 137, 140, 149, 178, 179, 182, 183, 188
Whipple, Joseph, 80, 81, 89, 90, 94, 99, 187
White Mountains, 8, 86, 87, 88, 89, 90, 92, 93, 96, 97, 99, 101, 111, 112, 184, 186
Winslow, Isaac, 64, 66, 166
Winslow, Maine, 52, 64, 66, 78, 130, 166, 190

Y

York, Maine, 3, 11, 12, 13, 14, 16, 28, 33, 55, 72, 77, 84, 86, 127, 147, 155, 163, 164, 165, 167, 168, 174, 176, 185, 186, 187, 188

ABOUT THE AUTHOR

Russell Lawson was born and raised in Tulsa, Oklahoma. His first intellectual interest was in ancient Greek mythology, which led to a lifelong fascination with the history of the ancient Mediterranean. He matriculated at Oklahoma State University from 1975 to 1979, majoring in history. From 1980 to 1982, he studied at OSU for a Master's degree in Ancient Mediterranean history. He earned a Ph.D. in American history from the University of New Hampshire in 1987. He lived in New Hampshire from 1982 to 1991, during which time he researched and wrote on New England history. He has taught at schools in New England, Oklahoma, and Ontario. Dr. Lawson teaches and writes on scientists, explorers, and missionaries; the history of America, Europe, and the world; and the history of ideas. He has written over a dozen and a half books. He is currently Professor of History at Bacone College. He is married, has three sons, and four rescue pups.

www.ingramcontent.com/pod-product-compliance
Lightning Source LLC
Chambersburg PA
CBHW071229170426
43191CB00032B/1204